POCKET
CALCULATORS

POCKET CALCULATORS

HOW TO USE
AND ENJOY THEM

Arnold Madison and
David L. Drotar

THOMAS NELSON INC., PUBLISHERS
Nashville   New York

First edition

Library of Congress Cataloging in Publication Data

Madison, Arnold.
    Pocket calculators.

    Bibliography: p. 135
    Includes index.
    1. Calculating-machines. 2. Calculating-machines—Problems, exercises, etc. 3. Mathematical recreations.
    I. Drotar, David L., joint author. II. Title.
    QA75.M32   1978   510'.28'5   78–707
    ISBN 0-8407-6580-0

For Helen Buckley Simkewicz
1 + 12 = 13

The authors would like to thank the following people for providing stimulation, service, and support during the preparation of the manuscript: William C. Ahearn, Pauline C. Bartel, Bruce Stephen Beckerman, Richard P. Drotar, Thomas B. Lyons, Donald E. Mack, Tom Moran, James V. Percent, and Fred Woodward.

CONTENTS

POCKET CALCULATORS

1

A MARVELOUS INVENTION

In Boston, Massachusetts, Gayle entered a store with her father, expectation making her tingle all over. Today was her birthday, and Dad had promised to let her select a pocket calculator as a gift. She wanted one just like the one her friend Susie owned. But as Gayle glanced at the shelves filled with small calculators and larger desk models, she became worried.

"What features do you want on your calculator?" the clerk asked.

Gayle shrugged. "I'm not sure."

"Certainly a floating point," the clerk said. "How about a memory?"

"Memory?" Gayle asked.

"Or maybe you plan on using only the four basic functions."

"What are they?"

The excitement had faded, and was now replaced by confusion. There just seemed to be too many different types of pocket calculators, and she did not know much about them. She couldn't even remember which company had made Susie's instrument.

Meanwhile, in Denver, Colorado, Ricky was studying the directions that had come with his new pocket calculator. The small slip of paper contained only brief instructions and some of them seemed totally unintelligible.

Ricky read a sentence aloud. "Transfers the displayed number to the memory positively (negatively)." He shook his head and read the sentence again. "Now what does *that* mean?"

In Mill Valley, California, Bobby was opening the front door, a skateboard tucked under one arm. His father called from the living room.

"Bobby, where's your calculator? I have some bills I want to total."

Bobby thought a moment. "I'm not sure, Dad. I think it's in my dresser drawer. I'll go look for it." He did not tell his father that he had not used the calculator for several months. After the first few weeks, there didn't seem to be anything new to do with the device.

These three accounts are fictional, but each day similar scenes are taking place all over the United States. People are entering stores to buy pocket calculators, only to find themselves perplexed by the vast array of them on sale. The directions supplied by the manufacturer are often obscure and hard to follow. A junior high school boy said, "People would prefer to read a logical book on calculators instead of the confusing directions that come with them." Once the initial excitement of owning a calculator wears off, a new owner often shoves the instrument into a drawer and leaves it there forgotten, because he has become bored doing the same things with it over and over.

Pocket Calculators is designed to help you if you are having any of these problems. Should you be considering the purchase of a calculator, then the chapter on how to choose and buy one would prepare you to shop intelligently. If you had trouble decoding the directions that came in the instrument's package, the explanations provided in this book should make operation easier. And if you feel you have already done everything you can with your calculator, you may be surprised by our suggestions on other ways to use it at home, at play, and in school.

The electronic calculator is a marvelous invention that might be compared to a tennis racket. In the hands of an untrained novice, the racket will send many tennis balls into the net. But in the hands of a pro, the same racket can produce wonders. And so it is with a pocket calculator. There are innumerable ways in which it can be a practical help, and it can also be a source of amusement in your leisure time.

Let's begin with a brief look at how this instrument, which has only been in existence since the late sixties, has now become a very popular household item.

2

THE HISTORY OF THE POCKET CALCULATOR

The pocket calculator can be traced back to a sun-bleached bone, as can the entire story of all counting devices. Even before recorded history, man knew how to count on his fingers, which explains why, today, our fingers and the numbers one through nine are both referred to as digits.

But what happened when the ancient hunter wanted to tally more than ten items?

He might have used his toes, of course, but somehow they are not as practical as one's fingers when arithmetic is involved. In all likelihood he snatched a whitened bone from the ground and drew lines in the hot sand. Sticks with etched notches became makeshift calculators, as did vines or ropes with knots tied in them.

As the people became more civilized, faster and more accurate calculating instruments were needed. The log is probably the means by which man discovered the wheel, thus paving the way for modern technology. Nature also provided the components of the first mechanical calculator, which would eventually produce the age of the computer.

As early as 600 B.C., an abacus may have been used in China. Another type of abacus was employed in ancient Egypt around 450 B.C. The first abacus was merely an extension of the cave man's sand drawings. Now the dirt grooves were used to hold small pebbles, which were pushed back and forth in the loose sand. Improvement came when the small stones were removed from the ground and placed in a wooden or metal tablet with carved tracks.

The modern abacus, which can be found as a toy in nursery-school classrooms and as a counting device in the Soviet Union and the Orient, has not drastically changed since ancient times. Today the abacus is usually contained within a wooden frame. Inside the frame are approximately twelve vertically arranged parallel wires or rods, which hold movable counters. Placed across all these rods is a divider. Usually one or two beads are on the upper side of this bar, while five indicators occupy the space below the rod. Each top bead stands for five while the lower markers represent one apiece.

The abacus is easy to learn and remarkably fast to operate. First, you *clear* the abacus by sliding all the 1-counters down and all the 5-counters up. The parallel rods, going from right to left, stand for ones,

The abacus is the oldest calculating device in existence. It is still widely used in Asia and the Middle East.

Courtesy IBM

tens, hundreds, thousands, and so on. To "write" the number on the abacus, you slide the beads to the center separator.

This very primitive arithmetic tool sounds archaic and hopelessly outdated, but it isn't. If you have ever visited a shop where the storekeeper is operating an abacus to total up the cost of several items, you probably stood in amazement as the counters clacked machine-gun fast against each other and the answer appeared almost immediately.

A further proof of the modern capability of this 2500-year-old digital calculator occurred in 1946. Man had moved into the atomic age, and there were individuals who felt that the time had come for the abacus to be retired to the status of another museum piece. An international contest was conducted, featuring a Japanese abacus operator and an American who manipulated a mechanical desk calculator. The abacus performed faster than the calculator in four out of five categories. The ancient counting device was not ready to relinquish its championship yet.

The abacus ruled supreme during ancient times and through the Middle Ages as the only mechanical counting instrument in existence. No advancements were made until 1642, when a French teenage mathematical and scientific genius, Blaise Pascal, finally initiated the next large step forward. He designed and constructed a mechanical adding machine, the Machine Arithmétique, which was driven by gears and had the ability to add eight-digit numbers. The basic concept of this seventeenth-century instrument can still be found in contemporary mechanical adding machines.

The Machine Arithmétique was the first real calculating machine. The stylus-operated figure wheels are so geared that a complete revolution of any wheel advances the wheel to the left one number. It is limited to addition and subtraction.

Courtesy IBM

The seventeenth century also witnessed the invention of a calculating device that became so firmly entrenched in scientific and mathematical circles that even in the twentieth century experts assumed the instrument would never become obsolete. William Oughtred is credited with devising the first slide rule, though the tool has been refined over the years by others. Even by the mid 1960's the slide rule and the abacus appeared unconquerable.

A major leap toward today's pocket calculator was taken in 1822, when England's Charles Babbage built his Difference Engine. This fiery philosopher and mathematician was compulsively driven to construct a mechanically operated device that would perform the four basic math functions: adding, subtracting, multiplying, and dividing. His Difference Engine was to be merely the first step toward a larger goal, because this instrument had limited usage in higher mathematics. Babbage's major goal was the Analytical Engine. The expanded capabilities of this proposed tool sound like today's computers and calculators. In addition to the four arithmetic functions, Babbage envisioned a device that would utilize punch-card input, have a memory of one thousand 50-digit numbers, and produce both visual and physical readouts.

Babbage slaved away at thousands of detailed diagrams that showed how to assemble the Analytical Engine and how it would operate internally. Unfortunately, man's vision far exceeded his technical talents. The component parts needed for the Analytical Engine would have had to possess hairline accuracy and simply could not be manufactured in the nineteenth century.

The idea for a Difference Engine that would compute mathematical tables, such as logarithms, was first conceived by Babbage in 1812. After twenty years of labor financial difficulties compelled him to stop work and the machine was never completed.

Courtesy IBM

For forty years, Charles Babbage worked on his Analytical Engine, but he died in 1871 without seeing his dream realized. His contributions, however, were major ones in the development of modern calculating instruments.

"If Babbage had lived seventy-five years later, I would have been out of a job." So said Howard Aiken, who, in 1943, with the aid of International Business Machines (IBM), produced the ASCC (Automatic Sequence Controlled Calculator). This complex digital calculator contained more than 3000 relays and could multiply two 23-digit numbers in four and a half seconds. Aiken had employed many of the principles developed by Charles Babbage as well as punched cards that could be read electrically. These cards had been invented by Dr. Herman Hollerith and were used as long ago as the United States census of 1890.

In 1946, Dr. J. Presper Eckert and Dr. John Mauchly developed a machine that signaled the beginning of the computer age. The Electronic Numerical Integrator and Calculator (ENIAC) was a scientific wonder, but its size made the production of an everyday calculator for the ordinary citizen seem impossible. The ENIAC contained 180,000 vacuum tubes, 11,000 switches and terminals, and more than 500,000 solder connections. Thirty months were needed to construct it and the immense machine occupied more than 1800 square feet of floor space. It operated about 180 times faster than the ASCC. Though the ENIAC was a significant achievement, few people could even imagine a calculator that was nominally priced and would slip into a person's back pocket.

During the next few years more machines were developed, each with ever-increasing capacities. The Electronic Delay Storage Automatic Calculator (EDSAC) was the first to employ a stored program, or memory. Then, in 1951, UNIVAC became a household word when the same developers of ENIAC, Eckert and Mauchly, produced the first modern digital computer, called Universal Automatic Computer I. The original UNIVAC was purchased by the U.S. Census Bureau and served them until 1963, when it was replaced by more advanced equipment. Subsequently, UNIVAC was placed on display at the Smithsonian Institution, Washington, D.C.

Science had moved rapidly after several thousand years of inertia, and was now producing machines with practically instantaneous calculative powers. However, the advancement toward a hand-held calculator as convenient as an abacus seemed nonexistent. Shoppers could buy small hand counters to total up their grocery bills, but these tiny devices could only add and had no memory. Actually, it was the bulky, room-sized computers that would enable manufacturers, at a future date, to produce wallet-sized electronic calculators.

Two other inventions were waiting in the wings, however, and when they walked into the spotlight, they had a profound effect on electronic instruments of all sorts.

In 1948, the transistor was invented. This device is similar to a vacuum, or electron, tube in function, but is much smaller in size. The most visible result of this invention were the portable radios, which suddenly appeared everywhere. And they really were portable

The room-sized computer actually provided the means for scientists to develop a pocket calculator.

Courtesy IBM

radios—no longer were they the size and weight of small suitcases, as before. Now people could be seen walking the street, holding a small box about the size and weight of a telephone receiver to their ears. The transistor also reduced the size of computers from a machine that filled a room to one that occupied as much space as a bedroom dresser. And, though the size of computers was reduced, their reliability improved when they became transistorized.

The development that would revolutionize calculators arrived in the late 1950's. Texas Instruments of Dallas, Texas, led us into semiconductor electronics with the introduction of integrated circuits. Fairchild Corporation, a few years later, improved these circuits further, and the miniature calculator was in its gestation period.

An *integrated circuit* is a complex of electronic components that can be fitted onto a single *chip*. A chip is a bit of crystallized, polished silicon containing up to 10,000 microscopic transistors. At first the chips were large compared to present-day chips and very costly to manufacture. The first pocket calculators appeared in 1971 and sold for $300. Further refinement of chip production kept lowering the price of chips from $30 to $20 to $5. Today, chips cost as little as 35 cents, and miniature calculators are now within the means of most people.

Other advancements took place as the popularity of small calculators grew. The first instruments had a fixed decimal point, so that the operator had to place the decimal in the correct location mentally. Now calculators have floating decimal points which, as the machine is operated, automatically adjust to the calculations and move into the proper spot. There is even a talking calculator on the market. "Speech Plus," produced by Tele-Sensory Systems, allows a blind person as well as the child with visual-perception difficulties to use a calculator.

Thus, scientific advance has created the second most popular electronic product ever brought to the consumer marketplace. Only color television sets have enjoyed more popularity, and they have been on the market since the 1950's. The pocket calculator is a child of the 1970's. Sales in a recent year totaled more than 40 million calculators.

This remarkable development, however, has exacted its toll in victims. Improvements in pocket calculators occurred so swiftly—within the brief period of only a few years—that many early purchasers of these devices saw their tools become outdated mere months after they bought them. Retailers often found themselves with many calculators in stock that had been replaced by cheaper and more efficient models. Often this meant selling the older calculator at a greatly reduced price in hopes of recouping some of the financial loss.

Open warfare exists on a large scale, even now among the manufacturers of calculators. Corporations rise in importance, causing the bankruptcy of others, only to be outclassed by another company and suffer their own decline.

Two other victims have fallen prey to the electronic age. That centuries-old fighter, the abacus, waged a gallant fight and gained our admiration through the years. But this is not 1946, and the abacus cannot compete with the operation of a pocket calculator. The slide rule, too, that white rectangle often sighted in university corridors and engineers' offices, has joined the abacus as something of the past.

Today, when people say calculator, they are most likely referring to the pocket calculator. The first thought of any one individual who is interested in such a tool is, "How do I choose and buy the right one?"

3

HOW TO CHOOSE AND BUY A POCKET CALCULATOR

The purchase of a pocket calculator can be a confusing task due to the myriad of types available on the market today. Department-store display cases are filled with rows and rows of the plastic boxes. All these calculators may seem alike to you at first. Yet each may be different in its respective functions and price.

Which kind should you buy?

Everyone should choose the pocket calculator that best serves his intended use. Individual needs will therefore govern the entire selection process, and, ultimately, personal taste will determine which model finds its way into your pocket. Knowing a few of the basics before shopping, however, will help you make a more informed decision. Nothing is worse than spending money on an item only to learn that it is not what you had really wanted.

Although technological improvements are continually being made in the electronics field so that the machine you buy today may be obsolete tomorrow, this fact should not influence your choice. The abacus, as already explained, has become outdated, but that doesn't mean all those calculating instruments manufactured before the computer age are no longer useful. Don't disregard a pocket calculator merely because the device does not contain the most recent improvements. If the instrument has the characteristics that best serve you, and you can use them with ease, then that model is a good buy. Also, you might be able to get a discounted price on an older machine.

An important question to ask yourself is, "What specific needs will my calculator have to serve?"

Pocket calculator characteristics can best be considered in terms of functions and features. A *function* is any mathematical operation, such as addition, division, or square root. The purpose of the pocket calculator is to perform the required functions. However, to make the task easier, several special features might be employed along with a function. A *feature* is any built-in characteristic or accessory device that aids in the operation of the calculator but does not by itself perform a mathematical function. The floating decimal point, which is fairly standard on most pocket calculators today, is an example of a feature. The floating point does not actually perform any computations. This indicator only helps the operator to understand the answer better.

Depending upon the desired functions and features, five different basic types of digital calculators are available. Before you decide which kind is right for you, be certain to familiarize yourself with the features offered by each one. The five types of calculator are: four-function, memory, slide-rule, scientific, and business.

The four-function calculator is by far the most commonly used type today. As the name implies, the four mathematical operations of addition, subtraction, multiplication, and division are incorporated into this instrument. This calculator can be purchased for as little as $5, and all indications are that the price may drop even lower. For tackling basic mathematical problems, the "four-banger," as it is nicknamed, is a workhorse. There are limitations to the four-function calculator, however, and, depending upon your needs, you may wish to purchase a more elaborate model.

When a calculator's capacity is expanded, so is the price. You should expect to pay more if more-advanced options are included. The memory calculator can do everything the four-function can do, but this machine can also store, or "remember," a number for later use. For example, suppose you solve a problem and want to use the answer as part of the next computation. The memory is a great help because you can enter the first answer into the memory and then recall that number when you need it for the second part. All these operations are accomplished without ever writing the figure on paper.

The third major classification of pocket calculators is the slide-rule calculator. Any function that formerly could have been executed on a slide rule can now be done on an electronic slide rule, with much greater accuracy as well as in a fraction of the time. Slide-rule calculators usually contain square root, square, and *pi*

The basic four-function calculator adds, subtracts, multiplies, and divides.

Courtesy David L. Drotar

keys. Most models also employ a special system called scientific notation. This feature is useful in the fields of physics, mathematics, and chemistry, where the numbers are often very large or extremely small and, hence, could not normally fit on the display.

For example, suppose someone wanted to enter a sizable figure, such as 93,700,000,000,000,000 into his calculator. The typical display panel could not show such a large number. But if the value is expressed in scientific notation, it becomes less cumbersome and much easier to handle. In scientific notation, this number is written as 9.37×10^{16}. The exponent 16 represents the number of decimal places to the right of the 9. In this way, the number can easily be both entered and read without attaching a string of zeros.

Another variety of pocket calculator, the scientific calculator, is generally most useful for college students entering such professions as engineering or medicine. Although pupils of high-school age or even younger probably would not have much use for the exotic buttons on this machine, a scientific calculator might be considered as a future investment if they plan to enter one of the above fields. In addition to using scientific notation, the setup of this model includes trigonometric functions, such as sine, cosine, and tangent. Logarithms are also available in this type of calculator. All these computations usually require long, involved tables, but the scientific calculator eliminates this need.

The last main subdivision of calculators, the financial or business model, contains such complexities as time and interest rates. Bankers, accountants, and

The scientific calculator is useful in the fields of engineering and medicine.———➤
Notice the exponents shown on the display.   *Courtesy King's Point*

Slide rule calculators contain square
root, square and *pi* keys
                    Courtesy King's Point

Memory calculators can store a number and
recall it at a later time. Key with M generally indicates memory capabilities. This particular calculator has the M located above
the key.   *Courtesy King's Point*

Complex business management is aided by the specialized functions of a ———➤
financial calculator.   *Courtesy Hewlett-Packard Company*

stockbrokers would have a need for these functions, but for the everyday money concerns of the average person, a simple four-function calculator would serve as well.

There are a host of other specialized types of pocket calculators being manufactured for various markets. But generally, even the most specialized types fall under the five main categories. In addition, be aware that a particular pocket calculator may possess a combination of the functions and features already discussed because the specifications of each type are not rigidly defined. A scientific calculator, for example, might have a memory but lack the scientific notation system. This crossbreeding makes it difficult to categorize a specific calculator.

Let's examine other features you should investigate when you wish to buy a calculator. Many salespersons are not fully familiar with all the features of the models they sell. Therefore, you should ask to see the owner's manual and perform several sample problems before purchasing an instrument. The operation of the device should not be so complex that you become confused. You are obtaining a calculator to simplify your work—not to create additional problems.

Strongly recommended is algebraic entry as opposed to the now outdated arithmetic entry. In algebraic entry, the numbers are entered into the machine in the same order you would write them. To solve $9-4 = ?$, you would press the 9, the minus $(-)$, the 4, and the equals $(=)$ buttons—in that order. Arithmetic entry has confusing extra steps. Certainly, you want to avoid any unnecessary procedures in your calculations. To distinguish between the two types in a store, check the keyboard. Arithmetic models have plus-equals $(+=)$ and minus-equals $(-=)$ keys, while algebraic types have separate plus, minus, and equals keys.

Most of the 160 million machines sold by 1977 had the preferred algebraic entry, but don't assume that a few of the other kind are not still available. Look closely so you won't be tricked into thinking the machine has algebraic entry when, in fact, the device possesses arithmetic entry. There is nothing wrong with the latter system. Just be certain of what you are buying.

One of the most important aspects to consider when buying a calculator is the keyboard. You should be able to manipulate the keys easily. Manufacturers have been producing smaller versions of their products, and, with the refinements in technology, several minicalculators are now on the market. Keys that are tiny and spaced closely may have an attractive appearance, but remember that human fingers will have to strike those keys. Science has not yet discovered a way to shrink hands. Keys that are too small and close can cause errors. Therefore, the keyboard's elements should be large and well spaced.

Since most calculator operators have a tendency to glance at the display when entering a digit, clicking keys might be helpful because they signal when a number has been activated. Also, they help avoid unnecessarily hard pressing. On the other hand, they could slow you down if you are entering many numbers rapidly. Also, with the resistance offered by the click mechanism, your fingers may tire more easily.

You might be considering a calculator that has the keys recessed into the keyboard surface. This may appear to be a good idea at first because an accidental keystroke would be prevented. But if the buttons do not protrude clearly above the keyboard, you might fail to enter a number because the proper key wasn't pressed down far enough.

Of equal importance to the keyboard in the selection of a calculator is the display: the small window in which the digits are illuminated. First, make sure you can see the display easily. You should be able to read all the numerals clearly and comfortably at a normal angle of use, which means the device should be flat on a table or desk as you sit behind it. The individual digits should be large enough to be seen well. Remember, however, that large digits drain the batteries and reduce the life of your power source. The display of a calculator, not the computations, expends the greatest percentage of battery power.

You have a choice of several different display colors. Numerals come in red, green, yellow, and orange. For most people, the bluish-green display is the easiest to see. And a fact worth considering when choosing a pocket calculator for yourself, or as a gift, is that a color-blind person may have trouble reading red digits in a display.

When you look at the display in dim lighting, even defective digits will be bright. The crucial test is to view the display in a well-lighted area. After final selection of your calculator, but before purchase, a wise action would be to test the exact machine you intend to buy. Punch in a full row of eights, as that is the only number that will tell you if every tiny line in the display is lighting up. Critically examine every segment and reject the instrument if all parts of each number do not glow with equal brightness.

The usual number of digits in a typical display is eight. Six- and twelve-digit capacities are also available. Six is really too few for practical purposes. The largest number that such a display could handle is 999,999. With an eight-digit display, the upper limit is increased to 99,999,999. If you anticipate working with numbers larger than this, a calculator with scientific notation would probably be better for you than one with an expanded display capacity of twelve digits.

A floating decimal point is a must in any pocket calculator. The operator can enter decimal numbers and view the answer with a properly positioned decimal point. Thus the greatest possible accuracy is ensured. You might want to consider a calculator that uses a fixed decimal point in addition to a floating one. The mode in which you wish to work, either fixed or floating, is determined by a separate switch. One type of calculator utilizes a fixed decimal point with two digit places following the decimal. This method represents dollars and cents as they are normally written.

The methods of powering the pocket calculator are varied and should therefore be considered when selecting your particular instrument. Batteries, available in penlight or nine-volt transistor sizes, are commonly used. Battery-run calculators are handy in schools, stores, and vehicles. Batteries have a limited life span measured in total operating hours, however, and must be replaced when they lose power. Alkaline batteries have a slightly longer life than ordinary carbon-zinc dry cells.

An AC adaptor is a useful accessory that can be purchased at the same time you buy the machine or at a future date. With the special adaptor, you can economically run the calculator from house current by plugging the cord into an electrical outlet. Whenever you buy an adaptor, be certain that the unit's voltage rating exactly matches the calculator's requirements.

Nickel-cadmium batteries are expensive to purchase initially, but over a long period of time, models operating on them will save you money. The AC adaptor/charger that comes with such calculators allows you to recharge the batteries and extend their use many times beyond conventional cells. And, if you want to become ultrafuturistic, you can spend a considerable sum of money on a solar calculator. Set this pocket-sized wonder in the sun and the device recharges itself for free.

There are also several pocket calculator features related to power consumption. If a calculator has a battery-level indicator, a symbol, such as an L, appears in the display when the battery power is weakening and the cells need replacement or recharging. This is a convenient accessory but not really necessary because the display would fade in brightness when the batteries lose power. Do not spend extra money to obtain a calculator with such a feature.

Another similar feature found on some instruments is a battery saver. The display clears itself if the number is illuminated beyond a certain length of time—approximately ten seconds. The action *will* prolong battery life, but having the numbers wiped out before you are finished using them could be annoying.

These calculators do have a special recall button, however, should you wish to retrieve the erased display.

A reliable power source is of little consequence unless the calculator casing is sufficiently rugged to protect not only the batteries, but the entire device. Durable plastic with recessed or concealed screws is preferred. You can easily spot shoddy construction yourself. If a manufacturer hasn't taken the time to produce a respectable exterior, then it is highly unlikely that the inside will contain quality electronic workmanship.

Many other features can be found on a pocket calculator, and they should be appraised in terms of what use they will be to you. Would a probe-operated wristwatch calculator be a novelty, only to be tossed aside later? Might you truly make use of a biorhythm calculator to determine your body's cyclical ups and downs?

Last of all, check to make sure that a dependable, no-risk guarantee is offered by the manufacturer of the calculator. A one-year guarantee including both parts and labor should be the minimum acceptable coverage. Do you or the store pay shipping charges if the calculator has to be repaired? Some retail stores might let you try out the calculator on a free fifteen-day trial basis. This period is not allowed so you can see if anything goes wrong with the mechanical components, but rather, provides an excellent way to determine if you are comfortable operating the machine.

Examine carefully every aspect of your intended purchase. All pocket calculators perform the four basic functions, but beyond that, they vary greatly.

4

HOW POCKET CALCULATORS WORK

All pocket calculators work on the numerous impulses of electricity that pass through them, just as televisions, radios, and other electronic devices do. But if you were to dismantle a pocket calculator, you might be surprised to find that there are few actual wires. Perhaps you may see several strands running from the battery connections to the main contents. Simply because a calculator lacks wires, however, does not mean that the instrument has no pathways for the electricity to follow. On the contrary, whenever a calculation is performed, electrical charges flow throughout the entire machinery along thousands of different routes.

Let's start with a simple math problem and trace the course the electricity takes in order to produce the answer that finally appears in the little window. During our electronic trip, we'll stop along the way to examine the various components of the calculator.

For example, you wish to add 4 and 3.

First, flip the main switch of the calculator. This activates the whole device and allows power to be drawn from the batteries, or from the house current if you are using an AC adaptor that plugs into an electrical socket. Generally, a zero appears in the display, indicating that the pocket calculator is operating. At this point the current is performing only one function; it is maintaining the single, lighted figure.

Next, punch three keys: 4, +, and 3. Finally, to get the answer from the instrument's brain, you press the equals (=) sign. During this process, you are operating the keyboard, which is merely a group of individual switches. Every key on the calculator is like a light switch in your home. The button turns on the power and sends the electricity to the right place. Unlike light switches, however, the power is stopped immediately after you press the calculator key. A small, springlike device under each key makes the button bounce back up, thus breaking the electrical contact.

What happens to these four electrical impulses that have been sent to the inner depths of the calculator? How does the electricity travel to all the right places if there are no wires to guide the signals?

The answer is a printed circuit board. A circuit is the path along which electricity can travel. The circuit board is a flat, cardboardlike sheet approximately the same length and width as the calculator itself. In manufacturing the printed circuit, a unique pattern has been specially drawn onto the board, using a conductive substance that will allow electricity to flow

The printed circuit board directs electrical impulses through its numerous pathways.

Courtesy Lawrence E. Abele

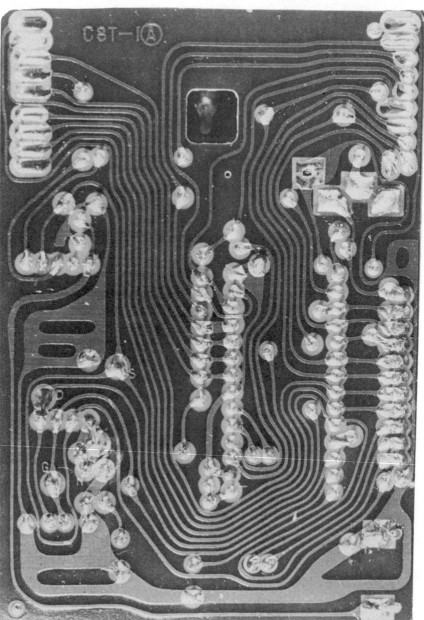

The all-important chip, the heart of the calculator, can be seen in this close-up photograph. The chip is the rectangular object labeled NEC. The chip is approximately three centimeters long.

Courtesy Lawrence E. Abele

through the material. The sheet is then coated for protection.

At this point, the figures entered into the keyboard are still basically in the same form as when we punched the buttons. The calculator must now do something with these numbers other than repeating them in the display. This transformation will take place when the electrical impulses are sent into the calculator brain: the chip.

As already mentioned, a chip, or integrated circuit, is a flat rectangular unit made from polished, crystallized silicon. The tiny piece is only a few millimeters long and weighs several grams, but it contains up to ten thousand microscopic transistors. If you looked closely at the chip's exterior, you would see several protruding metal "spider legs." These make contact with the printed circuit board. The inside of the chip is like a small version of a circuit board but, being more specialized, contains rather complex circuitry. An apt description would be to say the silicon chip is a tiny computer itself.

We shall now see what the chip's circuits do with the electrical charges that have entered them through the metal spider legs.

Stored inside the chip in the form of these circuits is a sequence of electronic instructions that process the information fed into them. We have entered two numbers, 4 and 3, and told the calculator to add them. The unique design of the chip accomplishes this by taking our coded electrical charges and combining them in a way that is built into the chip's structure.

Most chips can only add. The other three arithmetic operations are actually types of adding. To subtract, the chip mechanism makes use of the concept of negative numbers. A negative number is any number less than zero. A minus (−) sign is placed to the left, as in negative five (−5), for example. Subtraction is complementary addition, that is, addition of a number's negative counterpart. Multiplication is repeated additions, and division is repeated subtractions. Other operations, such as square roots and percentage are variations of the basic four. The same principle that governs the internal workings of a $5 pocket calculator also applies to the most expensive computerized system in the world today.

As one IBM engineer said: "Even the most sophisticated computers can only do four things: add, subtract, multiply, and divide. Everything else is derived from these four basic functions."

After the pocket calculator has computed the answer to our problem in the chip, its job is still not finished. What is it going to do with the result? Remember, the number is still in coded form: a spark of electricity sitting in a bunch of metal and plastic parts. If the calculator is to be of any use, the device must somehow give the answer in a way that we humans can read. To accomplish this task, the electrical charges are sent through the display register and finally arrive in the display.

Here, the current comes in contact with a chemical and causes the substance to glow. That is what you see when a number appears in the window. The ten numbers—zero through nine—can be formed by a combination of seven bars in the design of a divided rectangular-looking eight. The individual segments that are illuminated determine which number is produced. Each part of the digit is composed of light-emitting diodes (LEDs). At present, other types of displays besides LEDs are being developed, such as gas-discharge and liquid-crystal displays.

When there are several numbers appearing in the display, the calculator is really playing a trick on your eyes. All the numbers appear to be showing simultaneously. But that would drain too much power from the battery. Therefore, an electronic gimmick called multiplexing is employed. The digits are lighted individually in rapid succession, each one blinking off when the next one appears, which makes it seem as if they are all lighted at the same time. Multiplexing occurs so quickly that our eyes cannot perceive it.

There is a number in the display window of our fictional calculator right now. The answer to the 4 plus 3 problem that we entered into the instrument has been sitting there all this time. Though several minutes were required to read this account of how and where the impulses traveled, the actual process took only a fraction of a second.

The time span for the life of an average calculator is approximately four years, but with proper care, the device can and should last much longer. Neglect or abuse might mean repairs that could cost more than the original price of the machine. You can easily avoid damage to a pocket calculator, however, if you use common sense in caring for it.

If you keep in mind that the interior of the calculator is a delicate array of electrical parts, then you can understand that any type of physical shock could upset the mechanism. Obviously, you should take care not to drop the calculator or sit on it. But you should also be cautious about the way you place it on a desk or table top. Calculators are designed to absorb a certain amount of stress, but repeated shocks can have a cumulative adverse effect. When operating the calculator, don't strike the keys too hard, because that can loosen the circuitry. Apply light, even strokes as you press the buttons.

Treat the device as you would a good camera. When you are not using it, place the calculator in its carrying case. If you own an expensive camera, you will only open it to insert film. Certainly, you wouldn't touch the finely machined shutter. Follow the same rule with the calculator. The only time you need to open the case is when you change the batteries. Never touch the sensitive insides.

Several other basic precautions should be observed to ensure the proper functioning of the calculator. Don't forget to flip the off button when you have finished using the calculator. Such a warning may seem unnecessary, but it is very easy to walk away from the instrument after you have solved a problem, only to come back an hour, day, or week later to find that you neglected to hit that important switch. Calculators are silent and don't emit noise like a stereo

The figures in the calculator display are composed of seven segments.

Each segment is formed by groups of LEDs.   *Courtesy Lawrence E. Abele*

set, or heat up like a stove, which would warn you when they are still operating.

The batteries should be removed when you finish using the calculator, because cells sitting there for even a short period of time can leak acid and ruin the calculator components. Logically, it also follows that an AC adaptor should be unplugged whenever the calculator is not in use. The transformer in these gadgets can quickly burn out, leaving you with a worthless piece of cord and a wrecked calculator.

Although the calculator's circuits are not insulated, they can withstand a wider range in temperature than electronic devices that contain old-fashioned tubes. Vast extremes in temperature, however, should definitely be avoided for both storage and operating conditions. Don't leave the calculator near a radiator or in the sun or in such places as a hot car where the intense heat could melt the parts. You would be wise, also, not to store and especially not to use the calculator in temperatures that are below freezing.

Magnetism, radio waves, and electricity have similarities, so a few words should be said about calculator care in relation to them. Always keep the pocket calculator away from magnets or other strong magnetic fields, because interaction with interior mechanisms is unpredictable. Don't allow the device to pass through an airport's X-ray security check system; insist on a hand inspection.

So far we have concerned ourselves only with these sources of trouble that can influence the calculator. But improper calculator use can affect other devices as well.

The back of the calculator has been removed, and the device is opened book-fashion to reveal its compact interior. Battery compartment, upper left. Display, upper right. The chip is the rectangular piece with the letters NEC.

Courtesy Lawrence E. Abele

Just as a boat operator is responsible for the effects of its waves on other vessels, the calculator operator should be aware of the effect the instrument can have on other electronic instruments. An airplane's navigational and communications systems can be disturbed by the stray signals that emanate from a calculator. In order to avoid such interference, the use of a hand calculator aboard a commercial airliner should first be approved by a crew member. An ordinary AM or FM radio might also pick up signals from a calculator. This problem can usually be solved by keeping the units at least several feet apart.

Despite conscientious calculator care, malfunctions do occur occasionally in even the most reliable brands. If a problem should develop with your particular machine, it is important that you do not delay having the situation corrected. The defect could worsen and possibly damage other parts as well. Don't try to fix the calculator yourself. That might void the manufacturer's warranty. Any troubleshooting work should be done only by a qualified electronics repairperson. Check the guarantee that came with the calculator and return the device to the company in compliance with their instructions.

With proper care and sensible usage, however, your pocket calculator should serve you well. This relatively small electronic instrument is the result of a highly developed technology and is truly a masterpiece of scientific advancement.

5

OPERATING YOUR POCKET CALCULATOR

There it is: your brand-new pocket calculator on the table before you! The device has all the features and functions you desired and looks attractive with its tan case and black keys. You cannot decide what to do first.

First, become thoroughly familiar with this instrument, which can be employed for fun as well as for work. Read the directions carefully. Many companies use the same signs in their explanations as appear on the keys. Generally, a box will be drawn around the symbol so it more closely resembles the actual button. For instance, rather than stating, "Press the one key and then the add key," the instructions will read, "Press ☐1☐ and ☐+☐." These key symbols will be explained early in the printed directions.

The information sheet may give sample problems and indicate what numbers should appear on the display. Try their suggestions before doing your own. That way you will be certain to do a particular operation correctly. Immediately, invent several more examples and perform them. Repetition will help you to learn one procedure well before moving on to the next.

Acquainting yourself with your calculator means also being aware of its limitations. There may be printed suggestions on how you can care for it properly. Machines vary also in their scope. Find out what you cannot do with your model and how you can work around any operations for which higher-priced calculators have keys. For example, some models do not round off the last digit. If such is the case, be careful when using that answer for another problem. Your final outcome might be inaccurate.

This chapter will provide explanations for a number of operations. Some may be too simple or too complicated for your needs. Dip into the pages and select the most pertinent explanations.

Basic-Four Functions

Whether you wish to add, subtract, multiply, or divide two numbers, the steps are the same for all algebraic-type-entry calculators. You tap the number key(s) and then the function key and the other number key(s) and, finally, the equals (=) key.

Say you wish to add 22 and 108.

You switch the off-on lever to the "on" position. You

should see a zero in the display. If there are numbers, press the clear (c) button, which will erase them and give you the zero. Depress the 2-key. Now the zero is gone, and a 2 shows in the first right-hand digit place. Tap 2 again. A 22 is now in the display. Press the plus (+) button. To enter the second number, press the following keys: 1, 0, 8. Then you tap the equals (=) key, and the answer will appear in the display: 130.

Chain and Mixed Calculations

A chain calculation involves more than a two-step operation, and, therefore, each separate operation is like a link in a chain. An example of a simple chain calculation would be adding a column of numbers or multiplying three or more numbers. The most efficient way to do a chain calculation is simply to continue keying the numbers and the function alternately.

For instance, you wish to work this example: $25 \times 2 \times 5 \times 6 = ?$

Follow the steps you observed in computing the basic function. Clear the display. Enter 25 and tap the multiplication ($\times$) key. Then press 2, $\times$, 5, $\times$, 6 and, finally the equals (=) key. Your answer should be 1500.

Should your chain calculation be a mixed calculation, you will have to be a bit more careful. Perhaps you are presented with this problem: $3 + 6 \div 3 = ?$ There are two different ways to compute this, and they will result in different answers. If 3 and 6 are added, the answer is 9, which, divided by 3, would give you 3 as the final figure. However, if you divide 3 into 6 first, you will arrive at 2, which added to the first 3, gives an answer of 5.

Therefore, in a mixed calculation, unless the sequence is indicated, follow the "rules of order." These rules say that in any multi-step calculation, multiplications and divisions are carried out before any additions and subtractions. Returning to our previous example $3 + 6 \div 3 = ?$, we would do the division first and then the adding. To help us remember the order, we can place those portions that should be done first in parentheses. Thus, we could write this example as $3 + (6 \div 3) = ?$

Work $24 + (12 \div 4) = ?$ on your calculator and see how well you do. If you get 9 as an answer, you did not follow the rules of order or observe the clue offered by the parentheses. Do the division (or whatever is within parentheses) first. The correct answer is 27.

A more difficult form of mixed calculation is the use of parentheses and brackets. Let's say you are faced with $18 + [(8 + 4) - (9 \div 3)] = ?$ The procedure is to work the problem from the inside to the outside. Do the parenthetical portions first and then the bracketed section and, finally, the last step of the addition. Brackets mean second stage. First, you would add 8 and 4 and then divide 9 by 3. The two answers would be 12 and 3. Subtract 3 from 12, as the brackets indicate, and the answer is 9. Now do the final step by adding 9 to 18. Your answer is 27.

Now try one yourself. $17 + [(14 \div 2) - (3 \times 2)] = ?$

If you did not get 18 as an answer, check through your steps again. Did you do the parenthetical sections first, then the bracketed part, and, finally, the addition of 17?

Higher Powers

Occasionally, you may be faced with the problem of raising a number to a higher power. For instance, 10^6 means ten to the sixth power, or ten multiplied by itself six times. This would be a simple chain calculation. Work this example on your calculator. $3^9 = ?$ The display should show that 19,683 is the value of 3^9.

There is one more technique you may wish to learn, especially if you are going to be using your calculator a great deal. We might call the method "touch-calculating," like touch-typing. It means that the operator does not have to look at the keys. If you develop this ability for your calculating, it will increase your speed. The explanation will describe the procedure utilizing the left hand for the calculator operation. That way, if you are right-handed, you can write down the information. Should you prefer to do your calculating with your right hand, simply reverse the directions.

Some pocket-calculator manufacturers have simplified the task of acquiring touch-calculating skills by having a small bump on the five key. Check to see if there is one on your instrument. If your calculator lacks this, you can still touch-calculate.

Again, as in touch-typing, where your fingers always return to certain keys after striking others, the 4-key, 5-key, and 6-key will be the place to which you return—the home keys. Only the index, middle, and ring fingers are employed in touch-calculating. The ring finger should hover over the four, the middle finger over the five, and the index finger over the six. Place your hand in that position and you will notice that your thumb and small finger rest on the sides of the calculator. You can use them as a further guide that your fingers are above the correct keys.

Practice a few numbers, watching your fingers. Clear the calculator with the finger closest to the clear button, keeping the others approximately above the remaining home keys. Now strike the three, the six and the nine keys with your index finger. Clear the calculator. Go in the other direction. 963. Do this with each finger, striking the keys above and below the home key as well as that key. Repeat the routine over and over until you notice your speed increasing. Most people encounter difficulty manipulating their ring fingers. This seems to be the one that hits the wrong keys. You, too, may have this problem at first. But repetition will improve your skill with all fingers.

Now comes the test. Place a handkerchief over your hand, but do not obscure the display. Again, clear the board and do so before each finger is used. Tap in 369, 258, and 147. How well did you do? Go in the opposite direction and enter 963, 852, and 741.

Developing touch-calculating is merely a matter of practice. If you do the following exercise for half an hour every day for a week, you'll find you have perfected your skill. Write down about ten numbers. Have two-digit, and five-digit, and single-digit numbers interspersed throughout the list. Cover your hand with a cloth and see if the numbers are entered correctly. Work first for accuracy and then for speed. Take your time going through the column in the first attempts. Once you have gained accuracy, try to enter the numbers faster. Each day, when you return for practice, repeat this procedure, but have a different set of numbers. Remember: accuracy before speed.

Once you have fully memorized the number keys, use the same method for learning the function buttons. Different manufacturers place them in different areas, so you will have to adjust to your particular instrument.

This chapter has been a brief introduction to your calculator. There are many other ways to use the electronic device, both in school and at home—and some are sheer fun. Let us investigate first how a pocket calculator can help you become a better student and make school work easier and more enjoyable.

6

USING YOUR CALCULATOR IN SCHOOL

At a recent parent-teacher conference concerning her sixth-grade daughter, a worried mother spoke up. "If these kids are using pocket calculators in school, they'll never learn how to add or subtract. What will they do the day the calculator breaks?" she asked.

This sort of complaint has become increasingly common as more and more schools employ calculators in the classroom. The parents' fears are understandable, though baseless.

The National Council of Teachers of Mathematics, an organization composed of fifty thousand math teachers and thirty thousand institutions, has applauded the use of calculators in schools. "Mathematics teachers should recognize the potential contribution of the calculator as a valuable instructional aid. In the classroom, the minicalculator should be used in imaginative ways to reinforce learning and to motivate the learner as he (or she) becomes proficient in mathematics."

The key to the entire pro-and-con issue of whether or not calculators are good for you lies in those two words, *reinforce learning*. Do just that. Don't let your pocket calculator become a needed crutch, or otherwise you might very well be accused of carrying your brains around in your pocket. Use the device only to speed up, simplify, or check your work, never to replace sound thinking.

Teachers and school officials across the United States highly praise the pocket calculator and its effect on scholastic achievement. From nursery school to college, students each day are manipulating buttons and, by doing so, are learning faster and with more enjoyment.

Many people who previously could not or would not memorize the basic number facts are doing it faster and more accurately with the help of the calculator. Teachers are able to teach long division, fractions, and decimals at lower grade levels. Older children are employing deductive and inductive reasoning as they experiment with a calculator. By innovative thinking, students often learn new concepts that formerly had to be taught by lecture. In schools that utilize pocket calculators, math has become imaginative and fun.

Dr. Alexander Tobin, director of mathematics education for the Philadelphia schools, believes cal-

'Dataman' is a calculator-based learning aid to help youngsters seven years old and up to sharpen their math skills.

Courtesy Texas Instruments, Inc.

culators may even help schools save money in this time of increasing taxes. At first, the purchase of the instruments would appear to add more to a district's expenses. But schools do not buy calculators in classroom quantities. Frequently, a few calculators per room are sufficient. Dr. Tobin feels the instruments may help cut costs by "enabling slow learners to keep up with the class and requiring fewer special classes for those who otherwise couldn't master the various mathematical skills at the same speed as their grade. And students in special-education classes, who would normally be retarded in their math education, are able to learn the basic math facts."

As for the parents' fear that these students may not be able to function without a calculator, most schools that have the devices do not allow their students to operate them during tests. The evidence, even here, is firmly in favor of the pocket calculator. Those students who employ the machine regularly do just as well and sometimes better on tests than students who do not have access to a calculator.

Several mathematical computations will be explained in this chapter. But the calculator's use is not limited to math alone. A calculator can be helpful in other subjects as well, as you will see, and you will soon find even more ways in which your calculator can help you in school. But first, let us examine some mathematical ways to make a calculator work for you.

Finding Averages

Finding the average of a number of figures means arriving at a number that represents the typical number. Assume that you took four tests in science this marking period. You had the following marks: 85, 70, 96, and 81. You want to know your average in science for your report card. The average is found by adding up a column of figures and dividing the result by the number of items in the list. On your calculator you add the four numbers and find 332 to be your answer. Now divide that number by 4, because that is the number of figures you added. You should learn that your average mark in science this quarter is 83.

Changing a Fraction to a Decimal

There are certain common fractions for which we all know the decimal equivalents. For example, most people realize that ½ is the same as .5 and that ¾ equals .75. But what about ⅝? The rule for changing a fraction into a decimal is simple. Divide the denominator (bottom) of the fraction into the numerator (top). Using our calculator, we divide the 8 into the 5 and discover that ⅝ has the decimal value of .625.

Often we encounter a mixed number—a whole number and a fraction—such as 7⅝. To figure what this would be as a decimal, you use the fraction part only. Again, divide the numerator by the denominator. Jot down the whole number, place a decimal point after the figure, and write the readout showing on the calculator display. We learn that 7⅝ is 7.625.

Percentages

Many of the newer, four-function calculators have a percentage key. Should your machine not have one, you can still work percentage problems. Also, even if the calculator does have a percentage key, you will have to find some answers by other procedures.

Remember *percent* (%) means in proportion to one hundred. A percentage is merely a way of showing what relation exists between the part and one hundred. The whole is equal to 100 percent. Therefore, if you get ½ of the questions correct on a test, you have successfully completed 50 percent of them.

A typical problem you may be faced with is how to change a fraction to a percentage. Two steps are required. Say you have the fraction 4/5 and wish to know what it equals as a percentage. Step One: Divide the denominator into the numerator, and you will get a decimal number. In this case, you arrive at .8. Step Two: Take that decimal number and multiply it by 100; then write the percent sign after the answer. Actually, you do not need your calculator to do this second part. Multiplying a decimal by 10, 100, or 1000, etc., can be done mentally. You move the decimal point to the right the same number of places as there are zeroes in the multiplier. For instance, if you want to multiply a decimal by 10, just move the decimal point one place to the right. Should you be multiplying by 100, move the decimal point two numbers to the right. Multiplying .8 by 100 should produce the answer 80%.

To take percentage problems one step further, say you miss ten of the fifty-six questions on a test. You wish to know what percentage you had wrong. First, make a fraction by putting the part over the whole. The part is ten, which represents the number of questions you completed unsuccessfully. Put that over the whole, or fifty-six. You then have the fraction 10/56. Using your calculator, divide the denominator into the numerator, or the 56 into the 10. Rounding to three places, you should then arrive at .179 as your answer. Multiply that number by 100, or move the decimal point two places to the right. Your final figure should be 17.9 percent.

Perimeter and Circumference

Perimeter is the distance around the outside of a closed area. Utilizing the calculator to find the perimeter of any figure with straight sides is an easy task. Simply add the length of all the sides. The total will be the entire distance around the exterior of the shape. When talking about curvilinear figures, such as a circle, the distance around the outside is called the circumference. For example, the distance around the outside of a tree trunk is the trunk's circumference. Here the procedure is different but still simple for a calculator.

There are two more terms with which you should become familiar when considering circumference: radius and diameter. The distance from the outer edge of a circle through the exact center to the other side is called the diameter. Half that, or the distance from the center to the edge, is denoted by the term radius.

To determine the circumference of a circle, take your calculator and punch the buttons that represent the diameter and multiply that number by *pi*, or 3.14, which is the ratio of the circumference of a circle to its diameter. Therefore, if the diameter of a circle is 16 centimeters, you would multiply 16 by 3.14 and arrive at the answer of 50.24 centimeters.

Area

Area is the total surface enclosed within the boundaries of a shape, and the number is given in square units of measure, such as square yards or square meters.

Area of a Square or Rectangle. To determine the area of a square or rectangle with your calculator, multiply the length by the width. In a square, of course, all sides are equal in length, so you will merely square the figure representing one side; that is, multiply it by itself.

Area of a Triangle. The area of a triangle can be learned by multiplying one half the length of the base by the height. Remember, however, that your calculator does not work with fractions directly. You'll either have to change the ½ into a decimal (.5) or else divide the figure by two, which is the same as multiplying by ½. The base of a triangle may be any of the three sides. The height is an imaginary perpendicular line drawn from the apex, or the highest point of the triangle, to the base.

Area of a Circle. Once again you'll be using *pi* and the radius, which were explained above. To determine the area of a circle, multiply the radius by itself—thus squaring the number—and multiply that by *pi* or 3.14. Label your answer in square units.

Volume

Volume is the amount of space occupied by a three-dimensional object. This measurement is written in cubic units, such as cubic yards or cubic meters.

Rectangular Object. To determine the volume of a rectangular shape, multiply the length times the width times the height. Label your answer with the correct cubic unit.

Cylinder. A cylinder is a tube with a circular base. To compute the volume of a cylinder, we must obtain the area of its base. This is then multiplied by the height (length) of the cylinder. On the calculator you punch keys for *pi* (3.14) times the squared radius, then multiply that times the height. As with the volume of a rectangle, this figure is labeled in cubic units.

Reciprocals

A reciprocal is one of a pair of numbers that, when multiplied, equal 1. For example, the reciprocal of 5 is 1 divided by 5, .2. This is simple division for any calculator.

Negative Numbers

If you have to work with negative numbers, your pocket calculator should be able to do the job without any difficulty. All numbers greater than zero are called positive numbers. We do not usually put a plus (+) sign before them, however. As mentioned earlier, any number less than zero is a negative number and will have a minus (−) sign before it.

Say you want to add 7 and −8. Simply enter the 7, the minus (−) and the 8 into the calculator. Strike the equals (=) key and the display should show -1 as your answer.

The adding of two negative numbers can be done as quickly. Suppose you wished to add −8 and −8. You would tap the keys in the following order: minus (−), 8, minus (−), 8, equals (=). Your answer would be −16.

Negative numbers will be easy and fun to do with a calculator as long as you remember to key in the minus (−) sign before you enter each negative number into the calculator.

Square Roots

The square root (√) of a number is the number which, when multiplied by itself, will give the original number. The square root of 9 is 3. For 16, the square root is 4. Many calculators have a function key that will automatically compute the square root of a number. You enter the number and then press that key.

So you say your pocket calculator doesn't have a square root key? You can perform that operation, even with a four-function calculator. The process may take longer, but the result will be just as accurate. And when used with intelligent guessing, this procedure can be fun, and the time will be shortened considerably.

The number whose square root you wish to find should be divided by a reasonable approximation of the square root. Add the quotient (the result of this division) to your guess and divide by 2. This is the same as averaging the two numbers.

Now divide the original number by this average. Add the result to the previous average and divide by 2 to get a new average. Again, divide into the original number.

Repeat the process until you obtain two consecutive results that match. When you divide the original by the average and arrive at a number that is the same as the average itself, then you have found the square root. Use as many decimal places in your calculations as you wish your answer to contain.

Though it may sound complex, the whole procedure is very simple and can be thought of in basically only two steps: dividing and averaging. This is best explained with an example. Examine the problem below and then try finding the square roots of other numbers. Check an answer by multiplying the root times itself to give the original number. Remember—that is the definition of a square root.

Find the square root of 7569. Guess: 53

$$\text{Divide } 7569 \div 53 = 142.81$$
$$\text{Average } \frac{53 + 142.81}{2} = 97.91$$

Divide 7569 ÷ 97.91 = 77.31

Average $\dfrac{97.91 + 77.31}{2}$ = 87.61

Divide 7569 ÷ 87.61 = 86.39

Average $\dfrac{87.61 + 86.39}{2}$ = 87

Divide 7569 ÷ 87 = 87

The last two answers are alike. Therefore, the square root of 7569 is equal to 87.

Check 87 × 87 = 7569

Using these mathematical computations along with the basic four functions, you should be able to discover other ways for a calculator to help you in your daily schoolwork.

In science, for example, you may have a weather station in your classroom. The calculator will quickly provide you with the average temperature for the last month. Or, by checking a newspaper, you can obtain the temperatures of the major cities in the United States as well as foreign countries. Perhaps you would like to find the average temperature for the United States on a particular day.

If you are studying more advanced sciences, you may be analyzing substances to determine the percentage of their various components. Once you have finished the laboratory work, the mathematical aspect will quickly be accomplished by your pocket calculator.

More calculator assistance is available in social studies. Perhaps you wish to determine whether there have been more years of Republican Presidents or of Democratic Presidents. Computing distances in geography becomes much easier with a calculator on the desk top. Or, if you are doing an ecological study of your local area, obtain the pollution statistics from a county or state department connected with environmental protection. You could find the percentages of the different pollution types and even make predictions about which kinds of pollution will increase or decrease.

There are so many uses to which a pocket calculator can be put in school that several books would be needed to list them all. Unfortunately, in our time of rapid change, textbooks are not always up to date. Few, if any, of them include suggestions for calculator-related projects, so you must rely on your own inventiveness and on suggestions from friends and teachers.

There is another possible source of information about how to make your calculator a full-time worker, one that will make your school day more fun: a pocket-calculator club.

Pocket-calculator clubs for young and old alike are being organized in communities and schools across the United States. They can provide you with many enjoyable activities as well as increase your proficiency with calculators.

If you wish to form a club, find a faculty member or

parent in the community who will act as the adviser. A science teacher or a storeowner in your town who sells calculators might be interested in helping you. A student in Newhall, California, who helped create such a club, advises, "Don't get hung up with too much formal business. You're there to have fun with your calculator."

Here are a number of interesting and beneficial activities your club might consider:

- Have a sharing time. Members can bring magazine and newspaper articles or books related to calculators. Students may also want to describe some particularly good use they have found for the calculator, either in school or at home.
- Read some articles listed in this book's bibliography and construct some accessories for your calculator.
- Work together to build calculators from the kits currently on the market.
- Devote time to activities that will increase your speed and ability to operate a calculator.
- Organize teams and play some of the games given in Chapter 11.
- Volunteer your services and tutor slower math students in your school who are having problems with the subject.
- Contact other schools that have calculator clubs. You could arrange tournaments or share uses and projects for calculators.
- Prepare a newsletter for distribution in each classroom of your school. Alert other students and

teachers to the potential of calculator use in school.

- Invite guest speakers. Pocket-calculator salespersons could demonstrate new models or devices too expensive for you to purchase, but which would be fun to see.

Do give a calculator club some thought. Schools and communities that have them notice that interest usually does not lag, as can happen in other organizations. Usually membership and participation keep growing.

Continually growing, too, is the use of pocket calculators in schools. There is good reason. Students can learn faster when the drudgery is removed from their daily work. Also, new ways to incorporate calculators in all subject areas are constantly being developed. The calculator as a classroom tool is here to stay.

7

USING YOUR CALCULATOR IN LEISURE TIME

Besides having become an important educational tool, the pocket calculator can be put to a thousand uses in a person's leisure time. Leave the calculator in a handy place. If you are asking a telephone operator for information or hear a phone number on a radio or TV commercial, use the calculator as a note pad. You can tap the number into the calculator, faster than you can scramble for a pencil and paper. If your electronic device has a memory, you might even store the fact there for future use. Below are other applications for the calculator in the home.

Adapting a Recipe

With the large number of cookbooks published for people of all ages and the trend for boys to study cooking in junior high school, more and more young people are experimenting in the kitchen. Cookbooks can be helpful, but they cannot anticipate each user's needs. Often, therefore, you will have to adapt a recipe.

For example, you find a super recipe for a lima salad cup, but the directions will make six servings and you have eight guests including yourself. To figure how much you will have to increase the ingredients, divide the number of servings you want (8) by the number stated in the recipe (6). You will then learn that you must multiply each portion by 1.33. List down the makings and multiply each on the calculator to arrive at a recipe that will feed all your dinner companions.

Original Recipe (6 Servings)	Your Adaptation (8 Servings)
2 packages (10 oz.) frozen lima beans	$\times$ 1.33 = 2.66 or 2⅔ packages
2 cups sliced celery	$\times$ 1.33 = 2.66 or 2⅔ cups
1 cup cubed American cheese (from an 8-oz package)	$\times$ 1.33 = 1.33 or 1⅓ cups
1 pimiento, diced	$\times$ 1.33 = 1.33 or 1⅓ pimiento
¼ cup of bottled thin French dressing	$\times$ 1.33 = .332 or ⅓ cup

(Remember, you will have to change the fraction into a decimal before multiplying. This process was explained in Chapter 6.)

Should you want to use this same six-serving recipe for only four people, the procedure for modifying the amounts is the same. Divide the original servings (6) into the desired amount (4) and you will get .67. Now multiply each portion by .67.

Thus the calculator has made the process of adapting a recipe faster and more accurate.

Dieting

Americans have become acutely aware of the importance of maintaining their proper weight. Therefore, whether you are merely careful about what you eat, or are adhering to a strict diet, let your calculator count the calories. A word of caution. This book does not advocate any special diet, nor should you accept one because a friend followed a certain schedule and lost weight. Check with a physician to learn which diet is best for you and how rapidly you should lose weight.

Among the many diets available, there are two that are especially popular with young people. One involves limiting the total number of calories per day, and the other limits the carbohydrate intake in particular. Either of these diets can be used as a maintenance diet, which will hold your weight at a certain level, or a weight-reduction diet. In either case, your calculator will be a valuable tool.

If your doctor suggests you cut 1500 calories per day from a diet of 3000 calories, which would maintain your present weight, that leaves a 1500 daily calorie deficit. Divide that figure by 3500. It has been found that in order to lose one pound of weight, you have to reduce your food intake by about 3500 calories. Then multiply by seven in order to learn how much weight you will lose per week. This is the simple chain calculation explained earlier.

Daily calorie cutback ÷ 3500 × 7 = weight loss for one week.

The answer is 2.99, or about three pounds per week, in this particular case. This figure would not be appropriate for every individual considering a diet, however. Now you can take the weekly loss and divide it into the total number of pounds you wish to lose. This will determine how many weeks you will have to remain on your diet—provided you are disciplined. Not even a pocket calculator can give you self-discipline.

Whether you are following a low-carbohydrate, low-calorie, or another type of diet, you will have to plan your meals carefully. This can be a difficult task, because you will have to work out which foods you can eat if you are to avoid having too many calories or grams of carbohydrates. Which foods must you avoid, and what can you eat—and how much—to keep your diet on schedule? This adding and subtracting could be done with pencil and paper, but the process will be much swifter if you employ the calculator.

Electric Bill

If your family pays a monthly electric bill, your pocket calculator can be used for a little fun. The power company charges by the kilowatt-hour (kwh). The rate per kwh is usually stated on the bill. If not, you can figure the charge by checking a previous bill and dividing the kilowatt-hours into the amount. For example, you may learn that in your area, power customers pay three cents per kilowatt-hour. Listed on the bill may also be the date for the next meter reading.

Take a meter reading yourself on the same day the power company's reader arrives. If you are not familiar with your electric meter, you may be uncertain how to read it. There are usually five "clock" faces on the meter, containing the figures from 0 to 9. Each clock has a small movable hand which points at a particular spot on the clock face. Going from left to right, write down the number the hand has just passed. For instance, the first clock on the left may show 6, the next 5, then 9, 7, and 4. So your meter reading is 65974 kilowatt-hours. Check the last bill that arrived and note the previous meter reading. Subtract the old number from the present one, and you will determine how many kilowatt-hours your dwelling used in the last month. Multiply that by the rate per kwh. Add the sales tax for your locality.

When the envelope containing your family's electricity bill arrives, you can predict the amount before the letter is opened. If asked how you could possibly know, credit your success to ESP. The calculator won't tattle on you.

Carpeting

Perhaps you are redecorating your bedroom, or van. Some people use carpeting to transform their vans into comfortable living rooms on wheels. Find the length and width for each area you wish to carpet. If you are working on a van, this may include the walls and the ceiling—depending on how plush you want your truck to be. There are even vanners who carpet the inside of the back door.

Rug stores generally sell carpeting by the square yard, so you would be wise to do all your measuring in yards from the very beginning. Multiply the length times the width of each section. This will give you the area, as mentioned in the previous chapter. You will then know how many square yards you will need for each piece of carpet. By adding up all the square yards, or fractions thereof, you will get the total number of square yards you need for your van. When you shop for the carpeting, bring your calculator along. You will be given various prices per square yard and will want to use the instrument to help you quickly figure a total purchase price. Pocket calculators can be useful when it comes to comparative shopping.

Shopping

Many people carry a calculator along·while grocery shopping and enter each item as they place it in the cart. By doing this you will have a check on the accuracy of the market's cash register as well as being certain you have not exceeded the amount of cash in your pocket.

The calculator will also help you determine the unit pricing for different items. For instance, a 48-ounce jar of peanut butter costs $2.39. A 20-ounce jar of a different brand of peanut butter costs 64 cents. Which peanut butter is the better buy?

To shop wisely, calculate the unit price on your calculator. Divide the number of units into the price. In this particular case, the unit is an ounce. With the 48-ounce jar you will see that each ounce costs approximately five cents. The unit price for the 20-ounce jar is 3.2 cents per ounce. Obviously, the smaller jar is the more economical purchase because the peanut butter costs almost two cents less per ounce.

There is another way your calculator can be an ally when you invade the marketplace battleground. For example, a phonograph-record store that you frequent is advertising a 15 percent discount on all records. You select an album you like, which originally cost $4.95. How much will you really pay when the discount is subtracted?

First, you should transform the 15 percent into a decimal by dividing it by 100. This is the reverse of multiplying by 100, which you read about in the previous chapter. When changing a percentage to a decimal fraction, move the decimal point to the *left* the same number of places as there are zeros in 100. Therefore, dividing 15 percent by 100 gives us an answer of .15. Now use your calculator to multiply .15 by the price, which was $4.95. That will yield the answer of .7425, which rounds off to seventy-four cents. The final step is a simple one for your electronic calculator. Subtract $.74 from the price of $4.95, and you will find that this record will cost you $4.21.

Discount problems while shopping become complicated at times if you are not armed with a calculator. For example, if you were the vanner described earlier, you might find several choices of carpet: one that was being sold at a discount, and another, more expensive, carpet. If you buy more than 20 square yards of this second carpet, however, the price drops to one less than the discounted carpet. To determine the best buy without a calculator would be somewhat difficult to do while you were standing in the showroom.

Even if you are not carpeting a van, however, there are other uses for calculators in cars.

Automobiles

The nation as a whole is faced with the urgent need to conserve fuel. Use a calculator to determine the mileage of your or your family's car. Sometimes a trend of decreasing mileage can indicate a mechanical difficulty within the engine. The next time the gas tank is filled, jot down the number showing on the odometer. Let's say that figure is 16,573. Do the same when it's time to stop at the gas pump again, but also make a note of exactly how many gallons entered the tank. Suppose this time the odometer indicates 16,762, and the car needed 9 gallons of gasoline.

Now your calculator joins the action. Subtract the former mileage from the most recent one and divide that answer by the number of gallons. For our example, you would have this chain calculation:

$$(16,762 - 16,573) \div 9 = 21 \text{ miles per gallon}$$

Once you know how many miles per gallon the car is averaging, you will be able to help plan family vacations. Perhaps your parents are driving 476 miles to Milwaukee, Wisconsin, and you would like to estimate the cost of operating the automobile. First, check the cost per gallon of the type gasoline used in the car. Say that figure is 70 cents. All you do then is multiply the fuel cost per gallon times the distance divided by miles per gallon:

$$\$.70 \times (476 \div 21) = \$15.87$$

To help pass time on that long drive to Milwaukee, you can employ your calculator to estimate the minutes to a destination. Perhaps lunchtime has arrived, and the family has decided to eat at a diner in the next town. You see a sign, which says that that town is 35 miles away, and the car is moving at approximately 53 miles per hour.

How long will it be before you eat?

Click on the calculator and enter these facts: the distance divided by the car's speed multiplied by 60, the minutes in an hour. Now your chain calculation looks like this:

$$(35 \div 53) \times 60 = 39.6 \text{ minutes}$$

A pocket calculator can also be valuable when you want to double-check the reliability of a speedometer. Many automobiles presently on the road have inaccurate speedometers. The rear wheels feed the information to the speedometer, so if the tires have been changed or snow tires have been placed on the rear wheels, the speedometer may not be showing the true speed. To learn if the speedometer is in calibration, use a watch and your pocket calculator.

Many interstate highways have small signs posted exactly 1 mile apart from each other. If the car is driven at any steady speed from one sign to another and the number of seconds this requires is noted, you will have the information you need.

Divide the number of seconds into 3600, the seconds in an hour. Say the car used 68 seconds to cover that mile. Divide 68 into 3600, and you will see that your average speed was 52.9 miles per hour. If the speedometer indicated the car was moving at 45 miles per hour, there is almost an eight-mile-per-hour difference. This same automobile driven at the legal maximum speed would be moving about eight miles per hour faster. A highway patrolman will not check to see if the speedometer is in calibration before handing the driver a speeding ticket! And tickets are no fun.

Sports

Calculators can add even more fun to spectator sports. The next time you watch or attend a baseball or football game, bring along your calculator and figure up the game's statistics *before* they appear on the TV news. Or, if you've been following one particular team or player, you may want to acquire some information about the team's or the player's performance.

For many sports we talk about *averages,* when actually we mean percentages. For example, if you wanted to compute a person's or a team's batting average, you would actually be learning the percentage of hits out of attempts. The procedure is a simple one. Divide the total number of hits by the total times at bat. Work your answer to four decimal places and round back to the nearest thousandth. Of course, 1.000 is a perfect batting average.

The higher the number, the better the batting average, but for a pitcher, the lower the number, the better the earned run average (ERA). To evaluate a pitcher's skill, use your calculator. Multiply the number of runs yielded by that pitcher times 9, the number of players on a team, and then divide by the number of innings pitched.

Say a player pitches 6 innings and gives up 2 runs for that game. The following game, he surrenders 4 runs in 2 innings. For his final game, he pitches 7 innings and the other team gets 5 runs. Altogether he has yielded 11 runs. Multiply 11 by 9 and divide by the number of innings pitched—in this case, 15. This particular pitcher does not have an outstanding ERA. An earned run average below 3.50 is considered good. This person's ERA was 6.60.

Your pocket calculator can provide you with other information about sports. Perhaps you would like to know the average yards gained per pass for a football team. Key in the number of yards gained and divide that by the total number of passing attempts. Round off the answer to the nearest tenth.

Say you're a basketball fan and want to know either a team's or player's shooting percentage. Divide the number of baskets scored by the number attempted. The answer should be rounded to the nearest hundreth. To learn a player's average score per game, divide the number of points by the number of games played. Round this figure to the nearest tenth.

There are numerous sports-related activities for your calculator, and there are many other ways for it to make your leisure time more interesting and fun. The most important rule, perhaps, is to have the calculator always accessible. You have to break yourself of the paper-and-pencil habit. Soon you will be automatically reaching for the pocket calculator whenever some mathematical problem arises, wherever you are.

DON'T BE MUDDLED BY METRICS

Almost every country in the world today has adopted the metric system as the official method of measurement. The United States is currently in a transitional period. We are gradually replacing our old system of inches, quarts, and ounces with the universal meters, liters, and grams.

There is no need for confusion when dealing with metrics. You have probably studied and used the system in school, especially in science classes, and found it to be easier to work with than the old system of weights and measures. The most difficult part has been changing one system into the other, but now, with the aid of your pocket calculator, you can breeze through these conversions.

The best approach to take with any problem of measurement is to "think metric." Have a clear mental image of how long a meter is or how heavy a gram is. When you must change from one system to another, the procedure is simple. You can always find the equivalent of any given measurement by doing only one thing with your calculator: multiplying.

There is an appropriate conversion factor derived from the relationship between two units of measurement. If you wish to go from the old system to metric, there is a single number that will produce the metric equivalent if you multiply it by a specific old-system unit. The same is true when switching from metric back to the old way.

Length

Let's consider length first, since it is one of the first concepts we learn as a child. Big and small are two words that entered our vocabulary very early in life. But we're a bit more sophisticated now and realize that we can describe precisely how big, how small, how long, or how tall something is.

Suppose an art teacher asks you to buy a special type of drawing pencil that must be 5 inches long. What is this length when expressed in centimeters? From the proper section of the chart on page 91, you will discover that an inch equals 2.54 centimeters. Multiplying 5 times 2.54 on your calculator yields the answer: 12.7 centimeters.

Or perhaps you have just traveled 48 miles in the family car. How many kilometers is that? The chart tells you that to find kilometers when you know miles, you must multiply by 1.6093. Performing the computation 48 × 1.6093, you discover that you have gone approximately 77 kilometers.

All the charts in this chapter are self-explanatory and are designed for quick and easy reference. Each has been separated into two parts. The conversion of United States units to metric ones are listed first, and then metric units with their old-system equivalents. Symbols commonly used are given in parentheses.

When You Know the U.S. Units	Multiply by	To Find the Metric Equivalents
inches (in)	2.54	centimeters (cm)
feet (ft)	0.3048	meters (m)
yards (yd)	0.9144	meters (m)
miles (mi)	1.6093	kilometers (km)

When You Know the Metric Units	Multiply by	To Find the U.S. Equivalents
centimeters (cm)	0.3937	inches (in)
meters (m)	3.2808	feet (ft)
meters (m)	1.0936	yards (yd)
kilometers (km)	0.6214	miles (mi)

Volume

Although length is probably the most fundamental of all types of measurement, it is certainly not the most commonly used in today's modern household. Grocery packages are priced in terms of their contents' volume or weight, not by how long or wide the packages measure. Let's consider volume next. Another term for

volume when it is described in this context is capacity,
since we are speaking either of a liquid or a dry
measure.

Most food companies now list both old-system U.S.
and metric measurements on their products. For
example, the next time you drink a 12-ounce can of
Coke, notice the label. Does it also say 355 ml? Your
calculator can demonstrate the two figures' equivalen-
cy. Starting with fluid ounces on the chart, you find
that you must multiply by 29.5730 to find milliliters.
Punch 12 × 29.5750 = into your trusty calculator. You
will arrive at 354.9, or approximately 355 ml.

Maybe your sister just filled up the car's gas tank
before her weekend driving lesson with Dad. The tank
took 14.3 gallons of gasoline. Can you tell her how
many liters she purchased? Find the portion of the
chart concerned with changing gallons to liters. The
conversion factor is 3.7853. If you multiply 14.3 times
this figure, you will get the answer of approximately
54 liters. Sounds like a lot, doesn't it? Maybe if she
knew this, your swift sister would drive slower to
conserve fuel!

Your rich aunt living in France just came across an
utterly scrumptious new cheesecake and sent you the
recipe. No need to miss out on the dessert just because
the directions are given in metric units and you have
only old-fashioned measuring cups. The .5 liter of sour
cream called for in the recipe is easily converted into
cups. Can you do it on your calculator with the help of
the chart? Find the section that converts liters to cups.
The factor is 4.2268. When you multiply this times .5,
you arrive at an answer of approximately 2 cups.

When You Know the U.S. Units	Multiply by	To Find the Metric Equivalents
teaspoons (tsp)	4.9292	milliliters (ml)
tablespoons (tbsp)	14.7875	milliliters (ml)
fluid ounces (fl oz)	29.5730	milliliters (ml)
cups (c)	0.2366	liters (l)
pints (pt)	0.4732	liters (l)
quarts (qt)	0.9464	liters (l)
gallons (gal)	3.7853	liters (l)

When You Know the Metric Units	Multiply by	To Find the U.S. Equivalents
milliliters (ml)	0.2029	teaspoons (tsp)
milliliters (ml)	0.0676	tablespoons (tbsp)
milliliters (ml)	0.0338	fluid ounces (fl oz)
liters (l)	4.2268	cups (c)
liters (l)	2.1134	pints (pt)
liters (l)	1.0567	quarts (qt)
liters (l)	0.2642	gallons (gal)

Weight

There is one form of measurement about which Americans are especially concerned—weight. Every facet of our society is touched by it, and most of us are watching how much we weigh ourselves.

Are you tipping the scales at 127 pounds? Find your weight in kilograms. As usual, consult the handy chart. Finding the conversion factor to be 0.4536, you multiply your weight in pounds times this number and come up with a very slim 57.6 kilograms.

You are so grateful to your pocket calculator for instantly transforming you from a blimp into a shrimp that you decide to celebrate with a bowl of bran cereal.

The box contains 454 grams. What does this equal in United States measurement? Use your pocket calculator to translate.

When You Know the U.S. Units	Multiply by	To Find the Metric Equivalents
ounces (oz)	28.3495	grams (g)
pounds (lb)	0.4536	kilograms (kg)

When You Know the Metric Units	Multiply by	To Find the U.S. Equivalents
grams (g)	0.0353	ounces (oz)
kilograms (kg)	2.2046	pounds (lb)

Temperature

One other area that does not fall under any of the previous classifications deserves mention here also. Temperature measurements play an integral part in our lives, especially in weather forecasts and in heating our homes.

Increasingly, on radio and television, we have been hearing the outdoor temperature expressed in terms of the Celsius, or centigrade, scale. What does this mean?

Basically, the Celsius scale is a metric expression of heat and cold. However, the Celsius scale is based on 100 units. Water freezes at zero degrees and boils at 100 degrees.

To convert from Fahrenheit to Celsius and vice versa, use your calculator with the following formulas:

$$\text{Celsius} = (\text{Fahrenheit} - 32) \times 0.5556$$
$$\text{Fahrenheit} = (1.8 \times \text{Celsius}) + 32$$

Your friendly TV weatherman claims that the temperature will hit 29 degrees Celsius tomorrow. Should you invest in an Air Force parka or step out of the house in your swimsuit? Convert to Fahrenheit and learn the forecast in more familiar terms. Using the appropriate equation, we multiply 1.8 times 29 and then add 32. The result is about 84 degrees Fahrenheit, a balmy day.

The metric system is here to stay, and so are calculators. The two appear to have been made for each other. This compatibility has made calculator use fun while doing practical types of computations. Now, in the next few chapters, let's explore some of the more frivolous uses of the calculator: tricks, puzzles, and games.

9

TRICKS

When the developers of the pocket calculator were in the early stages of designing the instrument, little thought was given to anything other than practical uses. Even today, the functions and features of the machine are still geared for one and only one purpose—mathematical relationships. But sometimes numbers behave in strange ways, and, in combination with electronic wizardry, mathematics can indeed seem bizarre. Calculator users have discovered that their stolid devices can be used to perform a variety of unusual and amusing tricks.

Play the following stunt with someone and demonstrate your ESP abilities. Ask a friend to enter 98765432 into the calculator. Now tell him to divide by

8. Watch as the digits arrange themselves into proper ascending order, except for the divisor 8, which is deleted. The display reads 12345679.

Then, keeping the figure 12345679 on the display, ask your partner to name a favorite digit. If, for example, the person says 7, tell him to divide the number on the calculator by 10 and then multiply by 63. Miraculously, a row of 7s appears in the readout. The secret to the trick is simple. Always state the multiplier as 9 times whatever digit the person names. So, in the above example, you give 63 because the product of 7 and 9 is 63.

Here are some more number tricks that are especially fun for a mathematician to play on unsuspecting people.

Dwindling Doubles

Ask someone to think of any three-digit number. Have him punch the number into the calculator and repeat the entry. That is, if 483 was selected, the display should read 483483.

Now inform the individual that your psychic powers are telling you that the choice was very unlucky. Unfortunately, you state, that number is exactly divisible by 13. The division is computed on the calculator, and, of course, you are right.

"But wait," you continue. "It might not be so bad after all. I'm beginning to get some good vibes. Divide by lucky seven."

Your partner does so, and the result is still a whole number—not a decimal.

"Ah, that looks much better," you say. "I do believe, however, that you'd better not take any more chances. Quick! Divide by eleven before your luck runs out."

The person hastily makes the final computation, and his faith in your powers is reaffirmed. The original three-digit number reappears on the display panel: 483.

Sum-Thing

This feat is most impressive if you have a deck of playing cards available. Place a 6, an ace, and an 8 face down on the table. If this isn't possible, simply write the numerals 6, 1, and 8 on a sheet of paper.

Now have a friend think of any two numbers. They can both be either single digits or multiple digits or a combination of the two types. Ask the person to write the numbers in a column, one underneath the other, on a piece of paper, and to add them together.

Next, the sum (the third number down) is added to the previous number (second number) to get a new total. Again, this is written as the next entry in the growing list. At this point, the column should look like this:

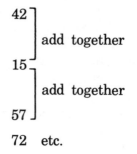

$$42 \left.\vphantom{\begin{array}{c}1\\1\\1\end{array}}\right\} \text{add together}$$

$$15 \left.\vphantom{\begin{array}{c}1\\1\\1\end{array}}\right\} \text{add together}$$

57

72   etc.

Continue in this fashion until there are twenty numbers on the page. Of course, the pocket calculator can be used for the adding when the numbers become large.

Instruct the individual to perform a division between the last two numbers. It does not matter which is divided into which. After the answer on the display has been checked, turn over the cards (or the original piece of paper). Your prediction will match the first three decimal digits on the calculator: 6, 1, 8.

How Old Are You Now?

Not only can you guess somebody's age with the help of a pocket calculator, but you can also correctly state the month and day of birth. Give the following directions to someone as that person keys the proper information into the system. But don't watch as it is being done.

First, instruct your friend to enter his birth date, both month and day, into the machine, using all numbers. The month is keyed in according to the following code: January = 1, February = 2, March = 3, etc. Then the day is entered, using two more digit places. A zero must precede any calendar day 1 through 9. For example, if your friend was born on September 5, a 9, a 0, and a 5 would be entered.

Next have him multiply by 2 and add 7. Then multiply by 50. Now say, "Add your age into the calculator and press the equals key." The subject will doubt that all these jumbled numbers could ever tell you the right answer.

Then take the calculator yourself and subtract 350. Your friend's birth date and age will be "written" on the display. All you have to do is translate them back into conventional format. The two places immediately to the left of the decimal point indicate age. The next two places toward the left will show the day of birth. And, finally, using the same number code explained above, the remaining one or two digits will represent the month.

Example: The calculator display would read 82610 for someone who was ten years old and born on August 26. Or 90106 would indicate that the person was six years old on September 1.

Masterminds Use 99's

You can take advantage of a unique property of the number 99 in this trick. Tell someone to choose a 3-digit number. Each of the three digits should be different. Now have the person write the number in reverse order, and to subtract the smaller number from the larger. If the original number was 479, then 479 should be subtracted from 974.

When the subtraction is completed, ask your partner to tell you only the first digit of the remainder. From this information you can predict what the answer will be when he divides the entire number by 99. The secret is to make your predicted number one greater than the number the individual tells you.

To continue with the above sample problem: 974−

479 = 495. The player would report the first digit as 4. You would increase this by 1, thus stating that 5 will be the quotient when the division is carried through. And 495 divided by 99 does, indeed, equal 5. There is one exception to the basic rule, however. If 9 is the first digit, your prediction should then be 1.

The Old Switcheroo

Before you approach someone with this trick, do a little preparation beforehand. Enter 27272727 into the calculator. Press the plus (+) key. Now enter 25252525, but don't press the equals (=) key yet. Cover that button lightly with your thumb, supporting the back of the calculator with your other fingers.

Keeping your hand in this position, hold the calculator in front of a friend. Tell your friend to concentrate on the display because the numbers are about to switch places at your command. Then, as you shout, "Switch!" gently squeeze your hand closed. At the same time, your thumb should depress the equals (=) key. The digits will rearrange themselves with a dizzying effect. The 2's and the 5's will have shifted positions so that the display now reads 52525252.

All the previous tricks in this chapter have been novelties that could be played *on* somebody. But the calculator user can also find entertainment when alone. If fact, you may get many surprises as you familiarize yourself with the various features of the device.

Several tricks to explore by yourself are described below. Let them be a starting point for further discovery into the world of mathematics. See if you can explain why they work. Using your pocket calculator as a tool to help you understand concepts can eliminate the drudgery from math and make it truly exciting.

Square Not?

Choose any number and square it. The square of a number is the product of that number multiplied times itself. The square of 4, for example, is 16. Your calculator might have an X^2 key. Or you might be able to accomplish the same function by entering the number and then pressing the times ($\times$) and the equals ($=$) buttons. You can always enter the number, press times, the number again, and, finally, equals. Find the simplest way to square a number on your particular calculator.

Now take the next-higher number to your chosen one, and square it also. Subtract the smaller square from the larger. Subtract 1, and divide by 2. You will end up with your original number.

Here is an example:

47 is chosen as the number
(1) $47^2 = 2209$
(2) $48^2 = 2304$
(3) $2304 - 2209 = 95$
(4) $95 - 1 = 94$
(5) $94 \div 2 = 47$

Roots

Select two numbers so that one of them is 5 greater than the other. Square both of them and add the two results together. Multiply by 2 and subtract 25. Now take the square root of your answer. Subtract 5. Dividing by 2 will give you one of the originally selected numbers. Add 5 to this number to get the other one.

Example:

Six and 11 are chosen as the two starting numbers.
Eleven is 5 greater than 6.

(1) $6^2 = 36$
$11^2 = 121$
(2) $36 + 121 = 157$
(3) $2 \times 157 = 314$
(4) $314 - 25 = 289$
(5) $\sqrt{289} = 17$
(6) $17 - 5 = 12$
(7) $12 \div 2 = 6$
(8) $6 + 5 = 11$

Now try this activity. Enter any number greater than 1 into your calculator. Push the square-root key, and repeat the action after each answer flashes on the display. You will notice that the numbers decrease in value with each square-root extraction that you make. Keep punching the button until you see that the roots have converged on 1. This point marks the end of the series because the square root of 1 is 1. You can not lower the value any more by taking the square root.

Now do the same trick again, except that after each square-root step, multiply by 2. Observe the result. The limit is not 2, but rather 4.

Try doing the exercise with 3 as a multiplier. The limit is 9. Repeat using several different multipliers. The limit always proves to be the value of the particular number squared.

Enter into your machine a number less than 1, but greater than 0; that is, a decimal number. Repeatedly push the square-root key as you did for the preceding examples. What do you find? How is the result affected when you use a multiplier after each step?

Almost, But Not Quite

"Just a little bit more."

"Nice try, kid."

"Almost, but not quite."

You've probably had a teacher say something like that to you, but have you ever witnessed it electronically? Do this trick and watch the numbers convey the same meaning.

A pocket calculator with a memory that you can add numbers into would be helpful, but isn't absolutely necessary. If you don't have this feature, simply record your results onto a sheet of paper as you work through all the steps, and then tally the numbers later.

Pick any number. Divide by 2 and add the result into the memory. Divide this new number by 2 and again enter the answer into the memory. Keep performing these repeated divisions and additions until you have exhausted the digital capacity of your calculator; that is, until division by two results in a decimal number so small that it registers as zero on the display. Now recall what has accumulated into the memory (or add together the numbers, if you have been dividing by 2 and writing the numbers down). How close is that figure to your original number? The number is almost, but not quite the number with which you started.

Once Isn't Enough

Multiply any 2-digit number by 3 and then multiply the result by 3367. Notice that your original number appears in triplicate across the display.

The mathematical mechanism behind this trick is revealed when you multiply 3 and 3367 together. Their product is 10,101. In this form, you can see that the multiplication steps in the trick were really equivalent to multiplying your original two-digit number three times, first by 10,000, then by 100, then by 1. The multipliers simply shift the original two digits into three different place values.

Example: Suppose you choose 96 as the two-digit number.

$$3 \times 96 \times 3367 = 969696$$

This is the same as $96 \times 10{,}101$

$$10{,}000 \times 96 = 960{,}000$$
$$100 \times 96 = 9{,}600$$
$$+ \quad 1 \times 96 = 96$$

$$10{,}101 \times 96 = 969{,}696$$

Calculator Five-O

Select any number and add it to the next-higher number. Then add 99 and divide by 2. Now subtract your original number. The result is 50. Repeat the trick with several other numbers. The final answer to this problem will always be the same no matter what number you choose.

Example: Choose 123.

(1) $123 + 124 = 247$
(2) $247 + 99 = 346$
(3) $346 \div 2 = 173$
(4) $173 - 123 = 50$

Would You Repeat That?

A repeating decimal contains one or more digits that occur in a fixed pattern over and over again. For example, numbers like .888888 or .494949 or .531531 fall into this class. Repeating decimals are easy to recognize on the display of your calculator and are fun to generate.

Here are a few. Perform the following divisions and note which digit or group of digits is repeated. Try to recognize an orderly sequence evolving with each succeeding division. As you go along, predict which numbers will complete the series and then use the calculator to check your predictions.

$1 \div 9 = ?$	$1 \div 99 = ?$	$1 \div 11 = ?$	$1 \div 37 = ?$
$2 \div 9 = ?$	$2 \div 99 = ?$	$2 \div 11 = ?$	$2 \div 37 = ?$
$3 \div 9 = ?$	$3 \div 99 = ?$	$3 \div 11 = ?$	$3 \div 37 = ?$
$4 \div 9 = ?$	$4 \div 99 = ?$	$4 \div 11 = ?$	$4 \div 37 = ?$
$5 \div 9 = ?$	$5 \div 99 = ?$	$5 \div 11 = ?$	$5 \div 37 = ?$
$6 \div 9 = ?$	$6 \div 99 = ?$	$6 \div 11 = ?$	$6 \div 37 = ?$
$7 \div 9 = ?$	$7 \div 99 = ?$	$7 \div 11 = ?$	$7 \div 37 = ?$
$8 \div 9 = ?$	$8 \div 99 = ?$	$8 \div 11 = ?$	$8 \div 37 = ?$
	$9 \div 99 = ?$	$9 \div 11 = ?$	$9 \div 37 = ?$

You can form other repeating decimals by taking the reciprocal (as mentioned in Chapter Five) of any two-digit number that is equal to 9 when its individual digits are added together.

10

PUZZLES

Pocket calculators are used everywhere in American society today—at home, at school, and in business. In fact, the device is becoming as common a household item as the toaster. It is only fitting that this ingenious tool, which was invented to simplify tedious work, can provide you with many hours of fun.

Experienced calculator users may already be familiar with an interesting property of the device—its ability to spell words. Due to the design of the seven-segment LED digits in the display, various numerals can be interpreted as letters when the display is viewed upside down. Enter .2578 into the machine and multiply by 3. Turn the calculator upside down and check the answer on the display. You will see an appropriate introduction to a whole new world of calculator capers.

Countless combinations of numbers can be made to resemble words by assembling the proper arrangements of pseudo-letters. For example, if it could fly and buzz your calculator might be called a "spelling *338*" (view the display upside down).
The digits and the nine letters they form are:

0 = O		5 = S
1 = I		6 = G
2 = Z		7 = L
3 = E		8 = B
4 = H		9 = G

By the way, did you know that even modern farm technology is making use of the calculator? Old MacDonald recently invested in a pocket calculator to keep an inventory of his chickens, pigs, and cows on the farm. Do the following problem and invert the displayed answer to find out what he says about the newfangled invention.

$$\frac{7 - 5.9496}{8}$$

Mrs. MacDonald, however, became extremely upset over her husband's new procedure of numbering all the cows instead of giving them names. But the shrewd farmer delighted his wife when he said, "Don't worry, love. You just stand on the other side of the pocket calculator and watch the display as I number that husky darlin' of a beast over yonder."
What did Mrs. MacDonald see when her husband recorded cow #315538?

In hopes of forecasting sales trends and thus increasing profits, a famous gasoline company installed monitors at each of their pumps. The individual units register gallons, price per gallon, and total price for each customer and feed these figures to a centrally based computer where they are added to the previous sales for the month. Suppose the pump devices recorded 32,689,417 gallons last week and since then 38,387,928 more gallons have been purchased by motorists. Find out the total number of gallons sold to date and at the same time find out (by reading the display upside down) who is responsible for initiating this system.

Now answer the following riddles or complete the sentences by performing the indicated calculations. See if you can guess the answer before actually doing the problem.

What kind of animal laid a 25-pound golden egg?
$$17504.959 \times 2$$
What does Santa Claus say when he comes down the chimney?
$$1.61616 \div 4$$
What do Santa's reindeer want for Christmas this year?
$$\text{a new } 231206 + 260169$$
Where does an Eskimo live?
$$5.65 \times .014$$
What surrounds a baby chick before it is hatched?
$$15466686 \times 5 + 12563$$
What does your mother tell you to wear when it is raining?
$$64561820 - 11111111$$

"And don't 225375 ÷ 5 in the puddles," she warns.
Water (6883 + 12153) × 3, but a steak 37605505 ÷ 7
when they are each heated on the stove.

What did the mouse say when it saw a human being
standing on top of a chair?

30 ÷ 9

Columbus is the state capital of 0.140 (enter directly). If this fact amazes you, you might say 501 × 9.

If you do this calculation correctly, the answer will
be a mistake:

(100.1 × 4) ÷ 5000

Disco Dinah dances to 600000 − 280992 music.

What is round in the middle and flat on both ends?

421 + 486

George Washington never told a 2536 ÷ 8.

You might fool Mother Nature, but you won't fool
the calculator. There are 0.370 (enter directly) calories
in five hundredths of a gram of butter, right?

You have two of them, but you never ought to be one.

12597 − 5263

Sometimes they jiggle, but they never jingle. And
they don't have zippers, but they do have buttons.
What are they?

2 × 2,658,869

Compute-a-Verse

Each of the numbers in the following poem can be
replaced by a word. Use the calculator to translate the
digits into rhyme.

There once was a creature named 9075
Who lived 'midst the muck of the 908.

It walked with a 378804
And spoke in a 378809.
When it ate it looked like a 904.

We have just seen in the previous puzzles how the calculator can be used to form words directly on the display. The machine's capabilities for word formation can be expanded further if we allow the digits to represent different letters. The words will no longer appear on the instrument itself, but instead must be written down on paper. In this way, we can use the digit combinations to decode blocks of information and construct whole sentences.

In the following puzzles, copy the problem on a sheet of paper. Then do the indicated mathematical operations on your calculator. Following the code below, decode each solution and fill in the blanks with the proper letters.

1 = A	6 = F
2 = B	7 = G
3 = C	8 = H
4 = D	9 = I
5 = E	0 = J

With this number-to-letter transformation accomplished, you will be able to read a complete sentence.

Here is a simple example to demonstrate the technique:

$$T \_ \_ NK \ W \_ L \_$$
$$(356 \div 4) \ (151 - 57)$$

Performing the computations, we get the numbers 89 and 94. The substitution of letters for numbers produces this gem of advice:

THINK WILD

Similarly, each of the following problems is solved in the same way.

$$\_ \_ R O L \_ \quad \_V \_ \_S \quad \_ L \ P \_ \_NTS \quad \_ V \_ R Y$$
$$(37 \times 22) \quad (7^2 \times 105) \quad (267888 \div 48) \quad (67 - 12)$$
$$\_V \_N \_N \_ \quad \_N \quad T \_ \_ \quad ST \_ \_M \_N \_ \quad \_UN \_L.$$
$$(5109 + 488) \ (3 + 6) \ (170 \div 2) \ (6000 - 803) \ (5 \times 0.15)$$

$$\_T'S \ \_LW \_YS \quad \_ \_ R \_ \_ R \quad \_ O M \_ N \_$$
$$(3^2) \ (693 \div 63) \ (45 \times 181) \quad (400 - 3)$$
$$\_OWN \quad T \_ \_N \quad \_T \quad \_S \quad \_O \_N \_ \ UP.$$
$$(\sqrt{16}) \ (3 \times 3 \times 9) \ (\sqrt{81}) \ (2 \times 4.5) \ (569 + 228)$$

$$\_U \_ \_Y \quad \_ \_M \_UR \_ \_RS \quad N \_ \_ \_ \quad \_ X T R \_$$
$$(3 \times 0.31) \quad (25 \times 3251) \quad (280 + 274) \ (102 \div 2)$$
$$\_ \_ \_ \_S.$$
$$(5 \times 7711)$$

$$\_ \_ \_ \_ \_ \_ \quad \_ \_ N \_S \ \_ \_ \_MON \_S \quad \_N$$
$$(888888 - 436593) \ (2082 \div 3) \ (3^3 \times 182) \quad (10 - 1)$$

$$\_R U M \_ L \_ N \_ \quad \_ \_ V \_ \_ S.$$
$$(300 \times 11 - 3) \quad (9 \times 35)$$

T _ _   _ _ R _ _ R   L _ _ T   _ _ S   _ _ _ _ R
(5 × 17) (56 + 2069) (7 × 8) (√7921) (26733 ÷ 7)
_ _ _RY.
(91 × 9)

R_ _ _   _ O R S _ S   _ R _ N _   _ N _ R _ Y
(1890 ÷ 14) (338 − 253) (125 + 669) (50 × 11 + 7)
_ N T O _ _ R T.
(4 + 5)   (7²)

The number code does not always have to be the same to work these word puzzles. Discover the next secret message by using the numerical representation of the mid-alphabet letters.

1 = K	6 = P
2 = L	7 = Q
3 = M	8 = R
4 = N	9 = S
5 = O	0 = T

_ H E _ _ _ U _ I _ _   _ _   _ _ _ _ U _ I _ _
(4 − 4) (2 × 476,027) (0.25 × 2) [(9,999,999 − 7,825,981)
× 3]
I _   D I _ U _ I _ _
(18 ÷ 2) [2000 + (6 × 9)]

You can see that it is possible to form coded sentences from a variety of letters and numbers. Try inventing your own. When you become good at it, you can send coded calculator messages to your friends.

Do you have a CB radio or a set of walkie-talkies? If

so, you and a friend can exchange messages over the air, without anyone else's knowing what the words are. After you receive the information, use your pocket calculator to translate the message.

Calculator Squares

In the number arrangements below, the total should be the same for each row, column, and diagonal. If you use your pocket calculator, you will discover the missing number quickly.

57	44	19
2	40	
61	36	23

333	434	463
540	410	280
	386	487

398		355
253	296	339
237	457	194

Here are some more complicated calculator squares. As before, each row, column, and diagonal adds up to the same sum.

182	32	148	106	37
86	50	135	55	179
49	180		22	153
23	147	67	152	116
165	96	54	170	20

In the next problem both missing numbers are the same.

188	45	143	86	163
123		180	72	106
83	94	125	156	167
	178	70	106	127
87	164	107	205	62

Can you find a logical pattern to the calculator squares? When you discover how they are put together, devise several of your own.

If you have worked through most of the examples in this book, you should be quite proficient in the use of the pocket calculator. You are now ready to enter into competition—the Grand Prix of mathematics. The next chapter contains several games that can be played with other people. Are you ready to accept the challenge? Got your calculator warmed up?

On your mark.

Get set.

Go. . . .

11

GAMES

The concept of recreational mathematics has been around as long as the abacus. Only recently, however, has the idea gained special impetus. Many colleges even offer courses that teach amusing games and delve into the theories behind the phenomenon. This surge of interest can be directly credited to the widespread use of the pocket calculator. The device has enlivened old standbys and is opening up whole new avenues of exploration.

But along with our desire for entertainment also comes a sense of competition. Each of the activities in this chapter involves playing the game with somebody. Unless otherwise indicated, the games can be played using only one calculator. Whether you win or lose the mathematical sport, we hope that the venture adds to your enjoyment and understanding of the calculator.

Less than Nothing

The object of this game for two people is to come as close to zero as possible, without ending in the negative.

The first player begins by entering any positive whole number. The person might choose 97, for example. The second player then subtracts from it any one of the single digits from 1 to 9. For instance, the second player taps the 4-key. Now 93 shows on the display.

After this initial subtraction, the game continues with the players' pressing any digit key (zero excluded) that is physically adjacent on the keyboard to the number last subtracted. So if 4 was played, the next player can only subtract a 1, 2, 5, 7, or 8. If 1 was pressed, then only a 2, 4, or 5 could be played on the next turn, and so on.

The game ends when a minus sign appears in the display. The player whose operation results in a shift into the negative range is the loser.

Play this game thoughtfully several times and you can develop your own strategy for winning. As long as the starting number is greater than 15, the player who makes the first subtraction can always win. Punch either 1 or 3 until the display reaches 13 or less, and then exercise caution with each succeeding move.

More than Something

Two people compete, each struggling to be the first to make the display read exactly 100.

The first player begins by entering any digit from 1 to 9. The next person must choose a digit that is in the same row or column as the previously entered digit. If, for example, the game began with a player's pressing the 7-key, the opponent must enter 8 or 9 (same row) or 4 or 1 (same column). This figure is added to the number on the display to arrive at a new total. The play continues in this fashion until the winner is declared by the deciding move, adding a digit that causes the total to reach 100. The display must read 100 and cannot exceed this value. If the final move results in a number greater than 100, then subtract 30 and continue playing from that point.

Scrazzle

As in the familiar Scrabble, the game of Scrazzle involves earning points for spelling words. Two or more people can compete. The Scrazzle board and pieces are all contained in one unit: your pocket calculator.

Chapter Ten describes how words can be seen on the display by viewing certain numbers upside down. Review those procedures again, if necessary.

The first Scrazzle player punches a word of any length into the calculator and passes the device to the next player. Using at least one letter from the previous person's word, the new player has one minute to think of a word and enter it into the machine. Five points are awarded for a word that is shorter than the former opponent's word, 10 points for a word of the same length and 20 points for a longer word. In addition, for every letter that exceeds the number of letters in the preceding word, 10 extra points are added to the score.

The game continues until the first Scrazzler to reach 250 points wins the game. Or, if desired, a total time limit for play can be set, such as 30 minutes.

Odd-It-Y

One of the players is selected as "It." The object of the game is for "It" to avoid becoming odd. "It" will strive to make the final number an even digit, and the opponent will therefore try to make it odd.

"It" begins the game by pressing any of the digits 0 through 9. Throughout the play, each digit can be used only once. A piece of paper with a list of the ten numbers might be helpful. As a number is played, it can be crossed off the list.

On the next turn, the opponent plays a function key and one of the remaining numbers. Division or multiplication by zero is not allowed. If a fraction appears, only one decimal place is considered in calling the result even or odd. 4.3672 would be termed odd because 4.3 ends in an odd digit.

The game progresses until each of the digit keys has been used once. If the final result on the display is odd, then "It" loses and must be "It" again. If, however, the number is even, then the other player becomes the new "It."

Example:

Player	Move	Display Reads
"It"	Enter 2	2
Opponent	− 1	1
"It"	+ 0	1
Opponent	× 3	3
"It"	× 8	24
Opponent	+ 5	29
"It"	− 9	20
Opponent	÷ 4	5
"It"	+ 7	12
Opponent	÷ 6	2

The result is an even number. "It" has won the game and the opponent must be "It" for the next round.

Pokulator

You don't need fifty-two cards to play this electronic version of poker. One calculator for each player is all that is necessary for Pokulator. Two or more people can play.

Each player enters a five-digit number (no 0's) into his calculator and then activates the divide (÷) key. The device is passed to the player on the left, who enters another five-digit number, and passes the machine back. The original holder now presses equals (=) to reveal his working numbers.

The seven digits to the right of the decimal point are used in forming the Pokulator hand. The player may discard any two digits of his choosing so that the best possible hand can be assembled from the remaining five numbers. Write the numbers on a piece of paper.

When all players have finished constructing their hands, consult the chart, which is arranged from highest to lowest hand. In the case of a tie between hands of the same type, the hand containing the highest numbers wins (for example, 55552 beats 44447).

Hand	Example
Five-of-a-kind	77777
Straight flush—even	02468
Straight flush—odd	13579
Four-of-a-kind	66662
Full house	88833
Even flush	64428
(contains only even numbers)	

Odd flush	97751
(contains only odd numbers)	
Straight	34567
Three-of-a-kind	22274
Two pairs	33669
Two-of-a-kind	44158

Sample play: You enter 75986 into your calculator and press the divide (÷) key. Your opponent enters 41237 and then you press equals (=) which results in 1.8426655 on the display. Ignoring the 1, your seven working numbers are 8426655. You would be wise to discard the two 5s and form this hand: 84266, an even flush.

Space Wars

Can you reach Planet PT–5 to capture the secret android before your opponent does? Put your galactic powers to the test.

You will need an interplanetary deck of cards. (If you haven't been shopping in space recently, an ordinary Earth deck will do. Simply remove the face cards, but not the aces.) And, of course, both space voyagers will each need a numeric synthesizer (pocket calculator).

The object of the game is to produce the all-powerful number 2001 on your synthesizer so that you can efficiently transport the spaceship. The following rules for the game have been adopted from the Official Galactic Congress on Space Travel to Planet PT-5.

Shuffle the deck. The first player begins by taking two cards and adding their values. This total is entered into the numeric synthesizer. The next step involves a number and a function, both of which are determined by drawing two more cards. One card will be the number and the other card will determine which function is to be used with the number. Follow this astral chart to find out which function may be used.

1 (ace)   any function (+, −, × or ÷)
2   +
3   −
4   ×
5   ÷
6   +
7   −
8   ×
9   ÷
10   any function (+, −, × or ÷)

You have drawn two cards and you are allowed to choose which one will represent the number and which one will determine the function. Suppose you draw an 8 and a 2. Letting 8 be the number and 2 the function, you would arrive at: + 8. This calculation is performed on the number already showing on your synthesizer screen. Alternately, letting 2 be the number and 8 the function, you might choose: × 2. The choice is yours. You can select whatever approach gets you to 2001 in the quickest way.

Players take turns drawing two cards at a time. If you exhaust the deck, return the cards, shuffle them, and use them over again. The first player to reach exactly 2001 wins the game.

Losing Sight of Your Goal

How good are you at keeping track of numbers in your head? This game for two people will test your ability to form quick, logical mathematical approximations.

Each player chooses a secret goal number and writes it down on a piece of paper. The object of the game is for the player to reach his goal number, while preventing the competition from reaching his.

Both players agree on a starting number and enter it into the calculator. Then the display is covered with a piece of tape or paper.

Now the players take turns executing any operation (+, −, ×, or ÷) with any number. The calculator is passed back and forth until one player believes that his or her secret goal number has been reached. The readout is unmasked and the players check to see how close the display comes to one of the originally written numbers.

As long as the result does not deviate from the goal number by more than 50, the person whose secret number comes closest to the display receives a point. If, however, the difference is greater than 50, no one receives a point, and the players begin a new round. The first person to acquire ten points wins.

Come to Order, Please

This game for two persons will require two calculators and a deck of cards. Remove the face cards and 10's from the deck, so that only aces and the 2's through 9's remain.

Now shuffle and place the first nine cards face down

in a straight row. Deal out the next eighteen cards of the deck to the two players—nine cards each—and discard the remaining cards. The players should not look at their "hands." Instead, they arrange the hands into single piles from which they can draw cards off the top.

The top card of each player's stack is exposed, and whoever has the highest number must make a decision. He can enter a 1 into his calculator or else choose the value of the first card in the row of cards dealt first. The hidden card is not revealed until after the decision is made.

The other player is forced to accept whatever remains, either the card or the number 1, and enter that into his calculator.

The number–2 position and all others up to 9 are played similarly, the player choosing between the number of that position or the value of the unrevealed card. For example, on the fifth position, a player could choose a 5, or he might wish to take a chance on getting a larger number with the card. Each succeeding result is added to the previous total. When all nine cards have been played, the totals are compared. Whoever has the highest number wins the game.

Variation: The game is played in exactly the same way, except that the low-scoring player becomes the winner. How will that affect your strategy?

Bingolator

This is a game for two or more players. If each person has a pocket calculator, that is fine, but a single calculator could easily be shared between players.

Each person requires a playing board like the one shown here:

1	2	3	4	5
6	7	8	9	10
11	12	13	14	15
16	17	18	19	20
21	22	23	24	25

They can be drawn on paper or cardboard, but be sure to make the squares large enough to hold a marker, such as a penny.

Four small slips of paper, with the symbols $+, -, \times,$ and $\div$, are mixed together in a hat or a bowl.

Now you are ready to play Bingolator.

All players begin by choosing any two numbers and jotting them down on a piece of paper. For example, you might select 8 and 3.

Next, one player draws a slip from the hat and announces the function that is written on it. Suppose multiplication ($\times$) was drawn. All players must enter their first number into the calculator, and perform the stated operation with the second number to arrive at a final answer. So you would calculate $8 \times 3 = 24$.

If the result matches a square on the playing board, then you are entitled to cover that section with a marker. In this case you would place a marker over the 24.

The slip of paper with the function is returned to the hat, and after everyone has written down two new numbers, a different player takes a turn at drawing again. The first player to get a row of playing squares filled, whether across, up and down, or diagonally, wins the game by yelling, "Bingolator!"

If you have several people who wish to play the game, one person could act as the full-time caller in order to speed up the play. That person would not participate in the board play, but would draw the slips of paper from the hat and call out the functions.

The truly smart Bingolator player will try to anticipate results according to the squares that are available on his board. For example, it would be foolish to choose 1 and 396 as your two numbers, since none of the numbers resulting from their addition, subtraction, multiplication, or division are even on the board. Luck definitely enters into this game, but skillful manipulation is essential to increase your chances of winning.

If you like this game, you might want to try some variations of the basic board pattern as set forth above. Devise several different boards with numbers of your own choosing. The game could also be played with different players using differently numbered boards. And possibly you might want to extend the play to fill the whole board rather than just a single row.

The games described in this chapter have been an introduction to a new sport: pocket gymnastics. You might equally enjoy creating your own calculator games and testing them out with your friends.

12

THE FUTURE OF POCKET CALCULATORS

The following statement appeared in a manual supplied with a new automobile: "The automobile has now developed to the point where it is not anticipated there will be further developments or changes, and this manual should be a reliable guide for the motorist of the future."

The car and the owner's manual were both produced in 1913.

People might fall into the same trap when discussing the future of electronic pocket calculators. The innovations that have occurred in the last few years have been so rapid and extensive that it appears there is no place for the calculator to go. In all likelihood, there will be changes not imagined at the present and, as has been true throughout the calculator's history, these developments may be introduced quickly.

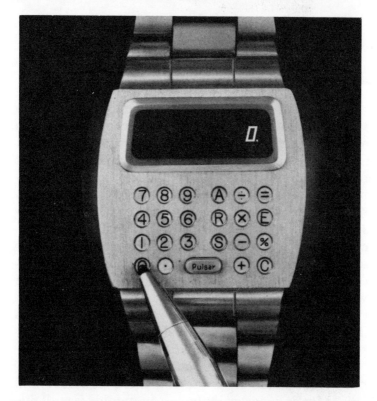

Electronic miniaturization has advanced to the point of producing an entire calculator inside a wristwatch.

Courtesy Time Computer, Inc.

One of the many varieties of calculators available is this carry-along calculator. The device is pencil-thin, a little longer than a ballpoint pen and an inch wide.

Courtesy Texas Instruments, Inc.

The success of today's calculator can be attributed to two factors: size and cost. There is even a wristwatch on the market with a calculator built into its workings. Several requirements, however, will not permit further miniaturization of the calculator. The instrument must be designed so that the keys can be manipulated quickly and without error, producing an answer that can be read with ease. Shrinking the calculator any further means the keys would be smaller and spaced more closely together. When the keys become excessively tiny, the calculator must be worked with a probe rather than fingers. This slows down the time required to make a computation. A miniature display is more difficult to read and therefore could be the cause of more frequent mistakes.

Battery size, however, can be reduced as improvements are made in producing more powerful and longer-lasting power sources. As liquid-crystal displays become more commonplace, the power drain will be reduced, so in terms of size, pocket calculators may become thinner in the future rather than smaller.

The cost of the pocket calculator may continue to decrease. Manufacturers may also begin providing more features on the less expensive four-function calculators without raising the price. Several corporations are experimenting in their laboratories with disposable calculators. Electronic counting devices that are cheaper to buy than repair would be a popular item in stores.

Other changes both minor and major may also be in the calculator's future. Possibly commas will appear in the display so that the figures will more closely resemble a written number. Or calculators will have a time mode that allows a user to compute time problems directly without converting to fractions.

Another development in relation to the display may be the introduction of alphanumeric characters: letters, punctuation marks, and mathematical symbols. There are accessories on the market today that can be connected to a pocket calculator, transforming the hand-held instrument into a desk model that produces a printout. These attachments are bulky and utilize a heat-sensitive paper that often lacks clarity. The pocket calculator of tomorrow may be the same size as the present device, yet produce a highly legible, solid readout.

Still another development may be an increased memory so that pocket calculators can be programmed much as computers are today. In fact, the greater use of microchips has permitted miniaturization of computer components and systems, which means that pocket computers may one day be available.

Another facet of the calculator's future lies in its impact upon our society. Already low-priced pocket calculators have reduced the drudgery of common mathematical operations. Everyone occasionally has the need to total columns of figures. Electronic counting devices within the financial means of most persons have greatly increased the accuracy and speed of such computations.

What other changes in our lives can we anticipate?

Perhaps a pocket calculator will be produced that is an electronic note pad. If memory and programming capacities continue to improve, we might be able to store telephone numbers, addresses, or important dates in our calculators. Simply jabbing a few keys would activate the pocket calculator into printing out the desired information.

Another suggestion that has been made is that the calculator could in some way be connected in your own home to a computer based elsewhere. Through it you could learn the times and places for school events or learn which stores are having sales on phonograph records. In this way, people could also obtain their telephone or electricity bills or determine their bank-account balances.

Fantastic, you say?

The pocket calculator even today is a fantastic instrument. The minds of men and women have taken counting devices from a bleached bone to a marvelous, hand-held electronic device. We can safely predict that scientific progress and imagination will lead us into a future where pocket calculators will perform even more wonders.

APPENDIX

POCKET CALCULATOR MANUFACTURERS

Bowmar/ALI, Inc.
531 Main Street
Acton, Massachusetts
01720

Casio, Inc.
15 Gardner Road
Fairfield, New Jersey
07005

Hewlett-Packard
Corvallis Division
1000 N.E. Circle Blvd.
Corvallis, Oregon 97330

Kingspoint Corporation
106 Harbor Drive

Jersey City, New Jersey
07305

Texas Instruments Inc.
P.O. Box 5012
Dallas, Texas 75222

Time Computer Inc.
HMW Industries
P.O. Box 1707
Lancaster, PA 17604

Unitrex of America, Inc.
689 Fifth Avenue
New York, New York
10022

FOR FURTHER INFORMATION

Rather than merely listing the books and periodicals that were used as reference material for this book, the authors felt the readers would like a more useful bibliography. The list below is divided into categories so that you can investigate other areas concerning calculators. If you are interested in more games, refer to "Calculator Activities." If you want to construct an accessory, look under the heading "Projects."

General Information

BOOKS

Mullish, Henry. *The Complete Pocket Calculator Handbook.* New York: Collier Books, Macmillan Publishing Co., 1976.

Roberts, H. Edward. *Electronic Calculators.* Indianapolis: Howard W. Sams & Co., Inc., 1974.

PERIODICALS

"Calculators: How to Keep Them Running," *Radio-Electronics,* 44:33–36, August 1973.
"Put a Computer in Your Pocket," *Reader's Digest,* 107:115–118, September 1975.
"Now—There's a Personal Calculator for Every Purse and Purpose," *Popular Science,* 206: 78–81, February 1975.

Calculator Activities

BOOKS

Arthur, Lee, Elizabeth Jones, and Judith B. Taylor. *Sportsmath: How It Works.* New York: Lothrop, Lee and Shepard, 1975.
Buckwalter, Len. *100 Ways to Use Your Pocket Calculator.* Greenwich, Connecticut: Fawcett Publications, Inc., 1975.
Frenzel, Jr., Louis E. *99 Ways to Know and Use Your Electronic Calculator.* Indianapolis: Howard W. Sams & Co., Inc. 1975.
Hartman, Arlene. *The Calculator Game Book for Kids of All Ages.* New York: The New American Library, Inc., 1977.

Judd, Wallace. *Games Calculators Play.* New York: Warner Books, Inc., 1975.

Mocciola, Dr. Michael R., and George A. Kreoll. *Calculator Activities for Children (ages 4–80).* Patterson, New Jersey: Numeral Press, 1976.

Mullish, Henry. *How to Get the Most out of Your Pocket Calculator.* New York: Collier Books, Macmillan Publishing Co., 1974.

Olney, Ross and Pat. *Pocket Calculator Fun and Games.* New York: Franklin Watts, Inc., 1977.

Schlossberg, Edwin, and John Brockman. *The Pocket Calculator Game Book.* New York: Bantam Books, Inc., 1975.

PERIODICALS

"Buying and Using a Pocket Calculator," *Popular Electronics,* 5: 62–4, May 1974.

"Computer Navigation for You," *Yachting,* 136: 43, August 1974.

"Ten Games," *Science Digest,* 77:42–45, May 1975.

"Calculators in the Classroom," *Today's Education,* 64: 42–44, November 1975.

"How to Make Use of a Mini-Calculator," *Mechanics Illustrated,* 71:40, February 1975.

"Calculator in the Gadget Bag," *Popular Photography,* 78: 100–101, May 1976.

"Fun and Serious Business with the Small Electronic Calculator," *Scientific American,* 235: 126–128, July 1976.

"The Calculator and the Curriculum," *Teacher,* Vol. 94, No. 6, February 1977.

Projects

PERIODICALS

"Teach Your Pocket Calculator New Tricks to Make Life Simpler," *Popular Science*, 205: 97—98, December 1974.

"How to Add Functions to Simple Hand Calculators," *Popular Electronics*, 8:38, September 1975.

"Build the Senior Scientist Calculator," *Popular Electronics*, 8:33, October 1975.

"Build This Electronic Stopwatch," *Radio-Electronics*, 46:43–45, November 1975.

"Theft Alarm for Handheld Calculators," *Popular Electronics*, 9:42, March 1976.

"Now You Can Build a Scientific Programmable Calculator," *Popular Electronics*, 9:36—38, May 1976.

"Build an Automatic Telephone Dialer," *Radio-Electronics*, 47:48–51, November 1976.

INDEX